Seeger, Raymond
    Men of physics: Benjamin
    Franklin, new world physicist

DATE DUE			
MAY 1 4 1991			
OCT 3 1991			

MEN OF PHYSICS

BENJAMIN FRANKLIN: NEW WORLD PHYSICIST

B. Franklin of Philadelphia L.L.D. F.R.S.

1763 Mezzotint of Franklin by Edward Fisher after Mason
Chamberlin, Philadelphia Museum of Art.

MEN OF PHYSICS

BENJAMIN FRANKLIN:
NEW WORLD PHYSICIST

BY

RAYMOND J. SEEGER
The George Washington University

PERGAMON PRESS

Oxford · New York · Toronto
Sydney · Braunschweig

Pergamon Press Ltd., Headington Hill Hall, Oxford

Pergamon Press Inc., Maxwell House, Fairview Park, Elmsford, New York 10523

Pergamon of Canada Ltd., 207 Queen's Quay West, Toronto 1

Pergamon Press (Aust.) Pty. Ltd., 19a Boundary Street, Rushcutters Bay, N.S.W. 2011, Australia

Vieweg & Sohn GmbH, Burgplatz 1, Braunschweig

First edition 1973

Library of Congress Cataloging in Publication Data

Seeger, Raymond John, 1906—
Men of physics: Benjamin Franklin, new world physicist.

(The Commonwealth and international library.
Selected readings in physics)
Bibliography: p.
1. Franklin, Benjamin, 1706–1790. I. Title.
QC16. F68S43 1973   530′.092′4 [B]
ISBN 0-08-017648-8   73-7981

60866

Printed in Hungary

In gratitude to

NORA ADELAIDE MADDEN SEEGER
AND
JOHN SEEGER

Contents

Acknowledgments

THE author and publisher are grateful to all who have allowed quotation from copyright material in this book. Their thanks are due to:

Royal Society, London, for permission to use the letter of 4 February 1750 from Benjamin Franklin to Peter Collinson.

Mrs. Richard D. Wood, Jr., Wawa, Pa., for permission to use the letter of 13 February 1757 from Benjamin Franklin to Jared Eliot.

Preface

THE twentieth century, despite its undermining of established intellectual foundations, has many characteristics in common with the eighteenth century, the so-called age of reason. The one distinguishing feature is the growth hof scientific technology and the interaction of technology and science; the former was accelerated by the industrial revolution in England at the end of the eighteenth century, the latter had its roots in the scientific renascence in the previous century. Recently the social byproducts of technological developments have become sufficiently magnified in their worldwide extension and urban intensification that man has become increasingly concerned about his *laissez-faire* economic and political policies. Too often he has been content to allow enthusiasts to pursue science for the sake of science in an artificial isolationism; now he realizes that all human activities can be permitted only in so far as they are at least for the sake of man—if not for a more universal reason.

It is enlightening to consider historically the early modern period when science, technology, and society were just beginning to interact under conditions qualitatively similar but less complex than those of today. The importance of an individual, enmeshed in his culture, is not to be discounted as merely a manifestation of it; there is a reciprocal relation in which the individual may become an important social factor. Such a person was Benjamin Franklin, who pursued an understanding of phenomena for their potential social utilization as well as for their personal intellectual satisfaction; moreover, he was a key link between Old World traditions and New World explorations.

At times, unfortunately, the fragmentation of our own early education and of our later specialization hinders our understanding of an integrated, many-sided personality like that of Franklin. Scientists, on the one hand, with short-sighted neglect of historical development and philosophical implications (involving people), frequently fail to appreciate even Franklin's contributions to modern physics. Humanists, in turn, with narrow devotion to a disembodied man, living independent of his environment, are often prone to neglect the role of his scientific interests in the very realization of his social goals. Undoubtedly we all need intellectual bifocals in our bifurcated academic culture, the more so as our imaginative powers become more rigid with fixed usage.

The present book is a simple invitation to focus one's attention once again upon Franklin as a physicist in the light of him as a person, to view the living humanism of science from its ever-deepening roots to its ever-spreading growth inward, outward, and upward.

Washington, DC   RAYMOND J. SEEGER

PART I
HIS LIFE

CHAPTER 1

Philanthropic Printer

BENJAMIN FRANKLIN, called the first American, was born January 17 (Old Style, January 6), 1706, in Boston, then a town of 5000–6000 population in the British colony of Massachusetts, which had been chartered in 1691 by William III (1650–1702) and Mary II (1662–94), out of the Massachusetts Bay (1629) and Plymouth (1620) colonies. He was fifteenth of the seventeen children sired by the "pious and prudent" Josiah Franklin (1657–1745), a soap boiler and tallow chandler, who had emigrated in 1683 from Banbury, Oxfordshire, England, about 7 miles west of Sulgrave, the ancestral Washington home. The Franklin family itself came from Ecton, a few miles from Northampton; it was typically middle class, enlightened by self-interest. His "discreet and virtuous" mother, Abiah Folger (1667–1752), from Nantucket, at 22 became the second wife of Josiah; the Folger family came from Norwich, England (1635). Their home was at 17 Milk Street, just across from the Old South Meeting House—symbolical of their puritanical background and outlook; their grave is in the nearby Granary Burying Ground.

Throughout his life Benjamin was prone to self-examination, particularly with respect to social obligations. He was sincere and honest; a man of affairs; he was shrewd and pragmatic. His ethics, however, were restricted largely to personal benevolence; his social concepts were somewhat reactionary. In 1776 he found himself quite in agreement with the economist Adam Smith's (1723–90) *Inquiry into the Nature and Course of the Wealth of Nations*. His moral concern resulted in personal economy (hardly frugality in his later life) and temperance (despite a secret youthful addiction to low women). His whole

3

life, which spanned the eighteenth century, was in keeping with its methodical discipline and reasonable order, with its sceptical abhorrence of superstition and hocus pocus, with its reliance upon sense and common sense, with its goal of human freedom and dignity. It was mitigated by an affable disposition. He was amiable rather than aggressive, with a good sense of humor and a ready wi'. He had a genuine joy in living; he liked good food but was not a gourmet; he drank rum and Madeira but did not smoke, chew, or use snuff. He was at home whether chatting at his own fireside, or joking in his club, or making love in a boudoir. He made lasting friends with persons of all ages.

Franklin was self-educated *par excellence*. Destined at the early age of 8 for the Church, he attended the grammar school later known as the Boston Latin School, where he became the head of his class. From the start he enjoyed reading, and throughout his life he remained an avid, powerful reader; at 82 he was wont to read in the bathtub. One is impressed with the breadth of his literary citations; Francis Bacon, Roger Bacon, John Bunyan, William Cowper, Horace, Thomas à Kempis, Cotton Mather, John Milton, Pliny, Plutarch, Alexander Pope, Pythagoras, François Rabelais, Isaac Watts, Xenophon—not to mention the Bible. The expected high cost and prospective low income of the ministry led to his transfer after a year to a George Brownell's school for writing and arithmetic, which he failed but mastered later by himself (a weakness, however, which persisted throughout life). At 10 he had to discontinue his schooling in order to assist in his father's business, where he acquired an interest and skill in handling tools. At 12 he was indentured as an apprentice to his brother James (1697–1735), who was a printer—a relationship equivalent to a trade school. Franklin always regarded himself as primarily a printer. At 82 he began his will, "I, Benjamin Franklin, Printer ... "—then only he mentioned his service as an ambassador.

Franklin devoted his Boston years to studies which prepared him for a journalistic career despite the nearby siren sea in which he became an adept swimmer. Ambitious to write, he systematically imitated the *Spectator* of Joseph Addison (1672–1719). His goal, then and later, was to achieve a style that was clear, smooth, and short. His first prose was a series of fourteen letters by a fictitious Silence Dogood; they were printed anonymously in the newly established (1722) weekly newspaper (the fourth in America), the *New England Courant*, published by his brother. These small efforts at 16 led to his being regarded later as the best writer in America in the eighteenth century; he is said by some to have established an American style of literature. Meanwhile, his apprenticeship to his brother inhibited his natural growth. He ran away. Today his statue stands in the yard of the Boston City Hall.

Failing to find suitable employment in New York City, by boating and walking he finally landed at the Market Street wharf of Philadelphia, then the second largest city (10,000) in the British Empire. Here, starting with one Dutch dollar and one copper shilling, he was to become a prosperous printer, a newspaper owner, and a good citizen.

In 1723 he became a journeyman for a printer, Samuel Keimer (1688–1742); he lived nearby on Market Street in the house of a carpenter, John Read (1677–1724). Franklin, who made friends easily, suffered on occasions from false acquaintances. Such a one was Sir William Keith (1680–1749), Governor of Pennsylvania, who promised him patronage but left him stranded without funds in London (700,000) where he had been sent on a mission. During his year and a half stay there he worked as a journeyman first with the printer Samuel Palmer in Bartholomew Close and then at the larger printing shop of John Watts (*c.* 1678–1763) near Lincoln Inn's fields; he lodged first in nearby Little Britain (once the residential section of the Dukes of Brittany) and then on Sardinia Street. He met interesting people such as Henry Pemberton (1683–1770), Gresham Professor of Physics and Newton editor, and Sir Hans Sloane (1660–1753), naturalist, later physician to George II (1683–1770), and president of the Royal Society, to whom he sold an asbestos (rare) purse. On his return voyage in 1726, Franklin formulated a life plan which he largely followed; it upheld frugality, industry, and truthfulness. He often hesitated to express an opinion, unless obliged to do so, for fear it might offend someone.

In order to pay back funds given him for his return trip, he was obligated to work in the store of a Philadelphia merchant, Thomas Denham (d. 1727). In 1728, however, he became a master printer and formed a partnership with Hugh Meredith (c. 1697–c. 1749); it was dissolved 2 years later. He opened his own shop near the market and courthouse, where he prospered for 20 years, owing largely to his innate charm and tactful persuasiveness—not to mention a systematic program of daily living and an excellent memory. In business Franklin was not only industrious, but also alert to opportunities; though slow to speak, he was prompt to act. He contrived the first copper plate for the reproduction of paper money (for New Jersey). In 1729 he bought and published the *Pennsylvania Gazette*, which he had conceived a year earlier. It turned out to be quite profitable and continued later as *The Saturday Evening Post, founded A.D. 1728 by B. Franklin*. He used it to publicize some of his own views, viz. defense of civil liberties and freedom of the press. In 1730 he became the public printer for Pennsylvania (with Meredith), for Delaware in 1734, for New Jersey and Maryland later. In December 1732 he published the first (1733) *Poor Richard's Almanack*, a humorous, homely product of a fictitious astrologer, Richard Saunders; in 1748 its sale amounted to 10,000 copies. A 25-year compilation of its best maxims, including proverbs sharpened by Franklin himself, was given as a speech by a fictitious Father Abraham in the preface to the 1758 *Poor Richard Improved* (the last one by Franklin himself); it was later published as the popular *Way to Wealth*. In 1743 he employed a Scottish journeyman, David Hall (1714–72), as a foreman; 5 years later they formed a partnership, which expired in 1766. Franklin's annual income from printing alone amounted to £500. He regarded as his technical "masterpiece" the 1744 edition of *Cato Major* (Cicero's *De Senectute*) by the statesman and scholar James Logan (1645–1751). On September 29, 1748, he retired from printing as a trade. He moved away to a new house at Race Street and Second Street, only to return to Market Street a couple of years later, and then a year afterwards to the Read area between Third Street and Fourth Street. He informed his friend Cadwallader Colden (1686–1776),

New York physician and political administrator, that he hoped now to have "leisure to read, study, make experiments, and converse at large with such ingenious and worthy men". In 1750 he wrote his mother that he preferred to live usefully than to die rich. He did both.

Although personally ambitious, Franklin was at the same time philanthropically minded; by virtue of his own character and experience he earnestly strove to improve the public welfare; he rarely sought an office, but was too public-spirited ever to decline one. As *Poor Richard* observed in 1757, "The noblest question in the world is, What good may I do in it?" Naturally gregarious, Franklin had an unusual gift for organizing activities. With nine others in 1727 he formed the Junto (corrupt for junta, viz. council) for common improvement—sometimes called the Leather Apron Club because it consisted mostly of tradesmen. It met initially in a tavern every Friday (for 30 years) to discuss humane and practical questions. In 1731 he organized the first circulating subscription Library Co. in the Junto quarters—his first project of a public nature. Its agent in London was a Quaker botanist and mercer, Peter Collinson (1694–1768), who purchased books including treatises on science and mathematics. The first order, in 1732, included Willem Jakob's Gravesande's (1688–1742) *Mathematical Elements of Natural Philosophy* (1726), Hermann Boerhaave's (1668–1738) *A New Method of Chemistry* (1727), Guillaume François Antoine de L'Hôpital's (1661–1704) *Analytic Treatise on Conic Sections* (1707). It soon had one of the best scientific collections in America. (At the time of his death Franklin himself had the best and largest (4000) private library; Logan's earlier library had about 3000 volumes.)

Franklin became an active member of the newly established St. John's Masonic Lodge in Philadelphia in 1731 and its grand master 3 years later; he was made grand master of the province in 1749.

In 1736 Franklin organized a volunteer Union Fire Co., and was instrumental in 1752 in starting the first American fire insurance company (the Philadelphia Contributionship). A year later he became postmaster of Philadelphia and was thus enabled to circulate his *Pennsylvania Gazette* more easily. In 1743 he wrote a circular proposal for promoting useful knowledge, somewhat broader than the Quaker farmer and royal (1765) botanist John Bartram's (1699–1777) inter-colonial scientific society suggested in 1739. The outcome was the American Philosophical Society (1744) with Franklin as its secretary. At the same time he suggested an academy for the youth of Pennsyl-vania to enable them to "study things that are likely to be most useful and most ornamental." It was to stress English rather than Latin (science had a minor role). A Board of Trustees of the Academy of Philadelphia elected Franklin (a life trustee) its president until 1756, when its charter was enlarged to include a college. The Academy opened in 1751; ultimately it became the University of Pennsylvania.

In 1747 Philadelphia was threatened by French and Spanish raiding privateers in Delaware Bay. Unfortunately, the Assembly was domi-nated by peace-loving Quakers and Germans as well as indifferent Scotch-Irish backwoodsmen. Franklin was inspired to write anonym-ously a dramatic appeal in an artful pamphlet, *Plain Truth by a Tradesman*. The response was favorable; a volunteer militia was immediately formed with Franklin playing an important role.

The physician Thomas Bond (1713–84) had proposed a Pennsyl-vania Hospital and sought Franklin's promotional skill through the Assembly and *Pennsylvania Gazette*. He secured the approval of the Assembly through his plan of matching funds. The corner stone of this first colonial hospital was laid in 1755, with Franklin president of its board.

Franklin's versatile professional and public life merged gradually with his private life to produce his ûnique personality. In 1771 at Twyford (near Winchester, England), the home of his friend Jonathan Shipley, Bishop of St. Asaph (Wales), Franklin wrote Part I of his *Autobiography* (for his son) in one week. It became a literary classic because of its simple writing about the daily concerns and intimate thoughts of a self-made man. He continued Part II in 1784, but had to stop and complete it in 1788, when he did Part III and began Part IV. What he finished covered only the first fifty years of his life. The original *Autobiography* was finally published in 1868. A representative portrait of the colonial Franklin is the one at Harvard, done about

1738–46 by the New Yorker Robert Feke (*c.* 1705–50). He dressed soberly and plainly (he was meticulous about his linen). He was just as much concerned about his reputation as about his character.

In 1730 Franklin married Deborah Read (1708–44), his landlady's daughter, whom he had courted upon his arrival in Philadelphia. Neglected during his London sojourn in 1725, she had married a potter by the name of John Rogers, who turned out later to have another wife elsewhere. He had disappeared in 1727 so that only a common-law marriage was possible. The Franklin's had a son, Francis Folger (1732–36), and a daughter Sarah (1743–1808). Both children were baptized at Christ Church. Sarah later married a merchant, Richard Bache (1737–1811); their son was named Benjamin Franklin Bache (1769–98). Meanwhile, Franklin acknowledged publicly an illegitimate son William (*c.* 1731–1813), who was appointed in 1763 royal governor of New Jersey and who remained loyal to the Crown (buried in Père Lachaise Cemetery, Paris)—to the chagrin and sorrow of his father. About 1760 in London, William, in turn, had an illegitimate son, William Temple (1760–1823), who was a close companion of his grandfather for many years.

Despite Deborah's refusal to go abroad, she was a faithful and helpful wife (he gave her a power of attorney in 1733). Her letters to him were always chatty and affectionate, even though she did not share his broad intellectual interests and social concerns. Franklin had a strong sense of family ties and obligations, bordering at times on nepotism. They are buried together in the Christ Church burial ground.

Although not especially spiritually minded, and by no means a churchman, Franklin devoted much attention during his life to religious matters. In 1728 he formulated for himself some *Articles of Belief and Acts of Religion.* In 1739, when the 24-year old English George Whitefield (1714–70) came bringing the Great Awakening to Philadelphia, he found the professional clergy closing the church doors. Franklin assisted in having a new building erected in 1740 for hearing a preacher of any religious persuasion and for certain educational activities (it was turned over to the Academy in 1750). In 1762 he assisted Sir Francis Dashwood (1708–81), Lord le Despence, prepare "An abridgment of the Book of Common Prayer." His sincerity is attested by his recommending on June 28, 1787, to the deadlocked Constitutional Convention that it apply "to the Father of lights to illuminate our understandings," inasmuch as "God governs in the affairs of men." The Convention took no action; probably, as Franklin noted, because it, "except three or four persons, thought prayers unnecessary." His deistic belief was best summarized a few weeks prior to his death in a letter to the Congregational minister and President of Yale, Ezra Stiles (1727–95); he regarded the moral and religious system of the man Jesus Christ as the best. He had, however, contributed to the support of the Presbyterian Church on Market Street, and he was a pewholder in the Episcopal Christ Church, which Deborah attended.

CHAPTER 2

Ingenious Natural Philosopher

FRANKLIN had a genuine curiosity about natural phenomena; he delighted in trying to understand them. He was never confined to a professional preserve restricted to advancing human knowledge for its own sake; in a strict sense he was an amateur, fortunately in an uncultivated field where simple techniques can yield great productivity. Franklin's investigations always exhibited acute observations, perceptive insights, ingenious experiments—and a determination to be bound by the facts. He was eager to communicate his findings with painstaking accuracy, but with little anxiety for personal credit. His expositions were simple and clear.

In the early days of the Junto one of his first queries, typical of his interest in daily experiences, was: Whence comes the dew that stands on the outside of a tankard that has cold water in it in the summer time? Franklin was fascinated by the quieting effect of a little oil on a disturbed surface of water. On his first trip to London he noted that the wakes of two of the ships were smoother than those of others. He was informed that the smooth wakes contained more greasy material. Later he himself experimented with oil on the Clapham pond (on the Surrey side of London). He used to carry a little oil in the upper hollow joint of a bamboo cane to make similar observations as occasions afforded. The phenomenon was later investigated on a larger scale at Portsmouth Harbor by Franklin and a few Royal Society colleagues.

On each of his trans-Atlantic voyages he showed keen interest in atmospheric and oceanic phenomena. In his journal for his first trip home (1726) he noted the appearance of a lunar rainbow, a lunar eclipse and a partial solar eclipse, Gulf Stream weeds, dolphins,

11

sharks, pilot fish, shell fish, grampuses, tropic birds, herons. On the third one (1775) he became the first to study the Gulf Stream which his cousin, Captain Timothy Folger (1732–1814) of Nantucket, had charted for him 7 years earlier; he took the temperature of the air and of the ocean several times daily. The following year he repeated his observations on his journey to Paris. And on his last trip to America (1785), at 79 he made similar recordings, including the ocean temperature at a depth of 18–20 fathoms. No wonder he supported Captain Charles Swaine's exploration (unsuccessful) of the Arctic in search of a northwest passage in 1753. He arranged safe conduct in 1779 for the English explorer Captain James Cook (1728–79) on his third voyage. In 1755, while visiting Colonel Benjamin Tasker (1690–1768) in Anne Arundel County, Maryland, he rode down the road after a funnel-shaped whirlwind until it became dustless and hence invisible. He was not content to watch the wind go by, but sought to penetrate its secret. Franklin expressed interest in strata of seashells in rocks high up on the Appalachian Mountains. He was puzzled by the fossil bones of a so-called mastodon dug up in 1766 at Big Lone Lick in Boone County near the Ohio River. In the *Pennsylvania Gazette* he discussed earthquakes and river colors, comets, and the aurora borealis.

A pot of molasses in his closet seemed to attract masses of ants. Could they possibly communicate with one another? He suspended the pot with one ant in it from a nail in the ceiling. When the ant had apparently eaten enough, it proceeded up the string and then down to the floor. Within half an hour the pot was swarming with ants, all of which left when the pot became empty. Pigeons came to mate in a box nailed to his house; always six pairs, never any more. Why? He built a box twice the size. Twelve pigeons occupied it. Franklin discussed agricultural experiments with a Connecticut minister, Jared Eliot (1685–1763). While in England he sent Bartram seeds for medicinal (Chinese) Tartarian Rhubarb, for Kohlrabi, for Scotch cabbage—all new to America. In 1775 he wrote to the Unitarian minister and chemist, Joseph Priestley (1733–1804; Copley medal 1773, discovered oxygen 1774; emigrated to Northumberland, Pennsylvania, 1794), about mash gas which could be set on fire in New Jersey, whereas he himself had been unable to kindle it in England.

His serendipity sometimes led to important developments. On October 21, 1743, he eagerly awaited an eclipse expected in Philadelphia at 9 p.m., but failed to see it owing to a northeast storm which had begun about 7 p.m. He later learned from a Boston newspaper that the eclipse had been visible there (400 miles northeast), where the storm had presumably originated. What was wrong? Franklin surmised that the path of the storm was not the same as the direction of the wind. Such a storm must have originated in the southwest, say the Gulf of Mexico—the beginning of man's understanding of cyclonic winds. Later (1783) he attributed the "dry fog" that covered Europe to volcanic dust. Two years later he noted that the fogs off Newfoundland were probably produced by the Gulf Stream.

It was, however, in electrostatics that Franklin made his most significant contributions so that he is rightly regarded as the outstanding American scientist of the eighteenth century. Sir Joseph John Thomson (1856–1940), winner of the 1906 Nobel prize for his discovery (1897) of the electron, the smallest electrical charge, claimed that Franklin was "a physicist of the first rank". Sometimes he has been compared with the natural philosopher and mathematician Sir Isaac Newton (1642–1727)—a judgment which has merit if one considers only the versatile Newton's non-mathematical approach to optical phenomena. Franklin's own involvement was somewhat fortuitous—but not his leadership in this field. He was ably assisted in his investigations by Ebenezer Kinnersley (1711–78), an unemployed Baptist minister, and, to a less extent, by the silversmith Philip Syng (1703–89), who invented an electrical machine (spheres rotating on an iron axle), and the lawyer Thomas Hopkinson (1709–51), who discovered the peculiar electrical behavior of points.

At Boston in 1743 Franklin met a science lecturer, Archibald Spencer (c. 1698–1760), a physician from Edinburgh and later a Maryland clergyman, who gave his demonstrations in Philadelphia the following year. His talk included electrostatic phenomena, the

English physician William Harvey's (1578–1657) theory of blood circulation, Newton's color investigations, *et al.* In 1746 the Library Co. received an electric green glass tube as a gift from Collinson together with instructions for its use. Franklin had duplicates made by a local glass-blower. A complete electric apparatus was later received by the Library Co. from the principal proprietor Thomas Penn (1702–75), son of the Quaker founder of Pennsylvania, William Penn (1644–1718). Now almost retired, Franklin set out at once to investigate these strange phenomena; in 1747 he reported his findings in letters to Collinson. He proposed to regard electricity as a fluid, not normally sensible. An excess, however, may be said to make a body positively charged, whereas a deficiency leaves it negatively charged— both states detectable as electrostatic phenomena. Implicit here is the modern principle of the conservation of electric charge, based upon a fundamental experiment regarded by the American Nobel (1923) physicist Robert Andrews Millikan (1868–1953), who first measured accurately the charge on an electron (1913), as "the most wonderful thing ever done in the field of electricity". Subsequent letters, on the basis of his simple conceptual scheme, explained the Leyden jar (so called by Franklin), initially a corked bottle, half full of water, with a wire through the cork into the water. It had been investigated first in 1746 by the Dutch natural philosopher Pieter van Musschenbroek (1692–1761), who advised Franklin in 1759 to "study nature, not books" (Franklin visited him in 1762).

In his July letter, Franklin particularly described the action of pointed metals. Two years later he compared the sparks from such points with lightning. Their properties seemed to be identical. Was lightning merely a grand electric spark? He suggested an experiment to test this hypothesis. In his notes he wrote, "Let the experiment be made!" It required an elevated rod. Franklin presumably delayed his proposed investigation until the new Christ Church steeple would be completed.

Meanwhile, a London physician and botanist, John Fothergill (1712–80), urged Collinson and Franklin to have the communications published in the *Gentleman's Magazine* published by Edward Cave

(1691–1754). The resulting book Experiments and Observaleone on Electricity (1751, with a supplemental Part II in 1753 and a Part III in 1756) has been regarded "the most famous and influential book to have come out of America in the eighteenth century". In that period there were five English editions, three French ones, one Italian, one German—but no American edition until 1941.

Sir William Watson (1715–87), a physician, reported favorably on this publication on June 6, 1751, to the Royal Society, of which he had become a member in 1741 and from which in 1745 he had received the Copley medal for his electrical research. Unfortunately, he omitted any reference to Franklin's important insight as to the action of a point and its applicability to protection from lightning.

A copy of the pamphlet came into the hands of the French naturalist George Louis le Clerc, Comte de Buffon (1707–88), director of the Jardin du Roi (now Jardin des Plantes). He advised a botanist, Thomas François Dalibard (1703–99), to translate it and to perform the suggested experiment. The latter did so on May 16, 1752, with a vertical iron rod (40 ft long, 1in diameter) in a Marly-la-Ville garden just outside Paris; his assistant became the first person to draw lightning from a cloud, i.e. sparks were drawn from the rod which had become electrified during a clap of thunder. A week later the experiment was repeated in Paris by a M. Delor, "a master of experimental philosophy". The well-loved King Louis XV (1710–74) had Abbé Guillaume Mazéas (1712–76) send a congratulatory note to the Royal Society. The experiment was successfully performed in England in July by the physicist John Canton (1717–82). In a month the Swedish physicist Georg Wilhelm Richmann (1711–53) was killed by lightning in experimenting with a rod at the Imperial Academy of St. Petersburg. During the same week in the very vicinity the Russian chemist Mikhail V. Lomonosov (1711–65) successfully performed a similar experiment.

Meanwhile, Franklin—apparently unaware of the work in Europe— performed (in June?) a modified experiment using a kite flying by means of a wet string—possibly on the outskirts of Philadelphia in order to avoid ridicule in case of failure. It was successful and was described in the October 19 issue of the *Pennsylvania Gazette*. Meanwhile, Franklin had encouraged Kinnersley to give lecture demonstrations throughout the colonies in 1751–2.

Franklin's accomplishment received worldwide acclaim. He was regarded as a new Prometheus who had stolen fire from heaven. In 1753 he received an honorary MA degree from both Harvard College (1636) and Yale (1701), in 1756 from William and Mary (1693), and in 1759 a LL D from the Scottish University of St. Andrew (1412) for his ingenious inventions and successful experiments; thereafter he was customarily addressed as Dr. Franklin. In 1767 he was awarded a DCL by the English Oxford University (*c*. twelfth century). He was the first foreigner (1753) to receive the Sir Godfrey Copley (d. 1709) gold medal for the "most important scientific discovery of contribution to science, by experiment or otherwise"—only 10 years after he began his scientific studies. In 1756 he was made a fellow of the Royal Society—the very group that had not published his letters in full because of supposedly insufficient merit. He was on its Council in 1760–1, 1766–7, 1767–8, and 1772–3. In 1772 he was elected one of the eight foreign associates of the French Académie Royale des Sciences (the next American to be elected was the Swiss-born Louis Rodolphe Agassiz (1807–73) one hundred years later). In 1781 he was made a member of the new American Academy of Arts and Sciences. By the end of his life he had been honored by membership in twenty colleges and learned societies (in America, England, France, Holland, Italy, Scotland, and Spain)—not bad for a school dropout!

In a letter to Colden in September 1749 Franklin confessed that he was "chagrined a little that we have hitherto been able to produce nothing in the way of use to mankind". In line with the view of the practical Sir Francis Bacon (1561–1626), in 1761 he remarked; "What signifies philosophy that does not apply to some case?" He did, however, recognize a developing period. A quarter of a century later in reply to a disparaging comment about the Paris balloon ascents of the Montgolfier brothers into the atmosphere, he retorted: "Of what use is a new-born baby?" (was he thinking of the two-week-old Ann Jay staying at his house?) He himself had an urgent desire to make his scientific knowledge immediately useful—contrary to the present widening gulf between science and technology in certain quarters. Franklin saw in science man's benefactor—contrary to a current tendency of some to regard science as essentially malevolent. Needless to say, it is man himself who determines whether anything, including science, is to be utilized for good or for evil.

Science, he confessed, "may help to make a vain man humble". Strangely enough, in 1785 he himself did not endorse the inventions of John Fitch (1743–98), who is regarded as the forerunner of the successful steamboat-builder Robert Fulton (1765–1815).

As early as May 1750 the *Gentleman's Magazine* printed his suggestion of using a pointed metal rod for protection against lightning. In September 1752 Franklin attached a bell to the lightning rod fixed on his own house to notify him of any electrification by passing clouds (depicted in Mason Chamberlin's (d. 1787) 1763 portrait of a thoughtful Franklin in his study). In 1753 *Poor Richard* had an article on. "How to secure houses, etc., from lightning" (the rod had to be firmly attached to the moist ground). In October he informed Collinson that the State House and the Academy already had lightning rods. In London, in 1764, St. Bride's, with its 234 ft spire—the tallest of the architect Sir Christopher Wren's (1632–1723) steeples, was struck by lightning. Five years later the nearby St. Paul's Cathedral was protected by lightning rods. Franklin himself never patented this device.

The lightning rod became a controversial issue. On the one hand, there were some religious objections to man's puny attempt to ward off the punishment of an angry god. On the other hand, some Tories had convinced George III that pointed rods were a Whig plot to attract destruction to government buildings. A Royal Society committee, consisting of the physicist Henry Cavendish (1731–1810), the mathematician John Robertson (1712–76), Watson, Franklin, and the portrait-painter Benjamin Wilson (1721–88; FRS. 1751, Copley medalist 1760), considered the question and recommended pointed rods—i.e. all except Wilson. Nevertheless, George III authorized blunt rods.

Wilson had painted Franklin's portrait in 1759; in this he appeared more refined in comparison with the previous American pictures. This portrait, hanging in Franklin's house in Philadelphia, was removed by Captain (later Major) John André (1751–80) when he was quartered there during the British occupation in 1777–8 under Major-General Charles Grey (1729–1807). The family of the latter returned it to the United States in 1906, where it resides in the White House— among portraits of presidents.

Franklin was a gadgeteer, ever making homely inventions as needs arose. In 1752 he devised a flexible catheter for his ailing brother John (1690–1756) in Boston. About 1742 he replaced the customary open stone fireplace with a more closed cast-iron stove which permitted fresh air to be admitted to the burning wood from the outside and then removed after passing through a firebox. This Pennsylvania fireplace (so-called Franklin stove) was never patented by Franklin. He designed also a three-wheel clock. At 82 Franklin made a mahogany chair with an accessible ladder beneath its cowhide seat; he also contrived a long arm to reach books on high shelves—later used in grocery stores. Probably best known are his Parisian, heavy-rimmed bifocal spectacles (1784), the upper half lens being less convex for distant objects, the lower half lens more convex for reading.

Franklin liked music; he learned to play the guitar, the harp, and the violin, as well as the so-called armonica. He also sang. In 1759 he modified the popular armonica to consist of thirty-seven glass hemispheres of different diameters, attached to an iron spindle controlled by a belt and treadle. With a light drum stick or finger, one could make the glasses vibrate (a three-octave keyboard was added later).

CHAPTER 3

Colonial Patriot

FRANKLIN'S prestige in science was a major factor in his political career. It was enhanced by his continuous correspondence with scientists whereever he happened to be stationed. A list of his correspondents reads like an excerpt from *Who's Who* in the eighteenth century: Bartram, the Italian experimental philosopher and Piorist Giovanni Battista Beccaria (1716–81), the Boston merchant and statesman James Bowdoin (1726–90), the French physicist Jacques Barbeu Dubourg (1709–79), Fothergill, the Scottish philosopher David Hume (1711–66), the Dutch plant physiologist and Vienna court physician Jan Ingenhousz (1730–99), the South Carolina physician (studied metabolism 1742) John Lining (1708–60), the Virginia physician and map-maker John Mitchell (d. 1768), Priestley, Sir John Pringle (1702–1782), Stiles, Whitefield, and the Harvard Hollis Professor of Mathematics and Natural Philosophy John Winthrop (1714–79). He was a friend of the best scholars in America, a vital link between the old world and the new. In 1756 he became an honorary corresponding member of the new (1759) London Society of Arts. He formed lasting friendships with young women who were charming and intelligent, notably the English Mary (Polly) Stevenson (1739–95), who married the anatomist and 1769 Copley medalist William Hewson (1739–74) and emigrated to Philadelphia in 1786; the English bishop's daughter Georgiana Shipley (d. 1805); and the Rhode Island Catherine Ray (1731–94), who married the jurist William Greene (1731–1809), later Governor of Rhode Island. His letters to Polly, from 19 years of age, have been regarded as a model of style (and of manners) in elementary science instruction. The urbane and versatile Franklin had an unusual talent for making and keeping friends of all sorts and conditions; he was a good listener and a good discusser, though a poor public speaker—he was, above all, a man of action. He had formed limited partnerships with printers in Charleston (1730), New York (1742), Antigua (1748), and Jamaica—all indicative of his growing intercolonial concerns, which marked his whole political career.

A successful and civic-minded tradesman, in 1736 Franklin became Clerk of the Pennsylvania Assembly (he is said to have doodled with magic squares during dull sessions; he was familiar with so-called amicable numbers) and in 1751 a Philadelphia representative in it; in 1748, now a rich and influential citizen, he was made a member of the Common Council and in 1751 an Alderman (until 1764). Having been Philadelphia Postmaster since 1737, in 1753, together with William Hunter of Williamsburg, he was appointed a Deputy Postmaster General for the Colonies by the Crown. His authority cut across colonial boundaries, he set out to improve the speed and safety of the mail. Henceforth he found some difficulty in balancing his loyalty to the people and that due to the king, which was aggravated by the proprietary feudal principles (less for William Penn in 1681 than earlier for George Calvert (1580–1637), Lord Baltimore, in the case of Maryland). The problems of Pennsylvania were further complicated by the growing metropolis about Philadelphia and the expanding Indian frontier—not to mention the concerns of the peace-loving Quakers, still powerful, despite their decreasing percentage of the population. Before Franklin, moreover, no one had done much to unite the colonies. He himself participated in the Indian pow-wows at Carlisle (1753). The French and Indian War began the following year. Impressed with the practicability of the Indian Confederation of Six Nations at the Albany Congress in 1754, Franklin, one of the two Pennsylvania Assembly commissioners, proposed a voluntary union of the northern colonies for mutual defense (and support)—not a single colony approved this plan, which was truly the beginning of American federalism. In 1755 Franklin had to assist the ill-equipped General Edward Braddock (1695–1755) by procuring 150 wagons and 259 packhorses from farmers for the disastrous march upon Fort

Duquesne. In view of frequent Indian attacks, Franklin, as head of an Assembly defense committee, journeyed with the militia to Bethlehem (founded by the Hussite Moravians in 1741) to build some forts. Even at the end of this war in 1763 the Treaty of Paris, in which France ceded Canada and all land east of the Mississippi as a result of James Wolfe's (1727–59) climactic victory (1759) on the plains of Abraham at Quebec, made no attempt to solve the inherent Indian problem. The Assembly selected Franklin as its special agent to seek redress from the king for the failure of the proprietors to contribute the funds requisite for an adequate defense.

Accompanied by his son, in 1757, Franklin arrived a second time in London ostensibly for a stay of 6 months—actually for 6 years (funded largely with his own money)—to plead for the civil rights of colonists as Englishmen. He lodged at 7 (now 36) Craven Street, the Strand, near Charing Cross (not far from the government offices in Whitehall). With his son and two Negro servants he rented four rooms from a good-natured and generous widow, Mrs. Addinell (Margaret) Stevenson (c. 1706–83). In the year following he began anonymously writing political material for London newspapers. He served as an energetic propagandist as well as a public relations man and a lobbyist. During this period Franklin was a staunch believer in the British Empire and in taxation with representation, which, he believed, could be achieved by better mutual understanding, possibly by a more direct liaison between the colonies and the English Government. In 1761 he attended the coronation of George (William Frederick) III (1738–1820), whom he then regarded as a virtuous and generous king. A year later he returned to Philadelphia and to a new house; he had to wait for a safe convoy because of the war with France. His son, about to marry a London beauty—despite an illegitimate son, William Temple (1760–1823)—returned shortly thereafter as royal Governor of New Jersey (and in 1766 he signed the charter of Queen's College, now Rutgers University).

The Assembly continued to have difficulties with the proprietors; in 1764 they sent Franklin back again to England, this time with a special petition to the king to assume the government of Pennsylvania.

Franklin became the agent also for Georgia in 1768, for New Jersey in 1769, and for Massachusetts in 1770. Upon his arrival, Franklin was confronted by Richard Temple Grenville's (1711–79) Stamp Act (1765) for official documents, a sequel to the 1764 Sugar Act. American boycott compelled its repeal in 1766. In this connection Franklin, as the voice of America, appeared for public examination before the House of Commons; he answered all questions briefly and lucidly; he stressed the mutual need for good economic relations between England and the American colonies. His request to return home after this success was not granted.

The Charles Townshend (1725–67) Revenue Acts of 1767 taxed co-lonial imports such as tea and aroused the colonies once more. The appointment of a Secretary of State for the colonies did not improve matters because of the unfortunate choice of Wills Hill (1718–93), Lord Hillsborough, from 1768 to 1822, who was quite different from the peers Franklin had met in the Royal Society. The maintenance of troops in Boston in 1768 at local expense, but without regard for local need, produced friction, and in 1770 sparked the so-called Bos-ton "massacre" (five killed). The Tea Acts of 1773, for the sole benefit of the East India Co., increased the tension further and led to the Boston Tea Party, at which sixteen citizens, dressed as Mohawk Indians, dumped tea chests into the harbor. Franklin deplored this lawlessness, and recommended colonial reparation. The retaliatory Coercive Acts (1774), which closed Boston Harbor, he regarded also as unjust and requiring immediate repeal. By now he had begun to suspect that the king himself was behind all these Acts of Parliament. The king, moreover, was indifferent both to trade and to science; so he naturally disliked Franklin who represented both.

The first Continental Congress (1774) sent a petition to the king to repeal these harsh measures being imposed upon the colonies since 1763 without any representation at court. Franklin presented it to the new Colonial Secretary, William Legge (1731–1801), Earl of Dart-mouth (after whom Dartmouth College was named in 1769). Mean-while, another storm had been brewing; it started with certain letters written by Thomas Hutchison (1711–80), Governor of Massachusetts, when he had been Lieutenant Governor in 1767 and 1769. They contained inflammatory comments such as "There must be an abandonment of what are called English liberties". The letters had been sent to Boston for private circulation, but were seized upon by colonial agitators as evidence for the desirability of having the governor deposed. On Christmas day, 1773, Franklin admitted that he himself had been the unknown transmittor of the six documents to Boston in 1772. He was summoned to appear before a committee of the Privy Council on the following January 11. Upon his appearance he was made to stand in silence for an hour and listen to a sarcastic diatribe by the Solicitor General, Alexander Wedderburn (1733–1805), Earl of Rosslyn, who represented Hutchison. The committee rejected the petition for removal, and the Privy Council approved its action. In disgrace, the scapegoat, Franklin, was summarily dismissed as Deputy Postmaster General. His departure from England was hastened by news of the death of his wife. He returned to Philadelphia on May 5—after Dartmouth had ordered Lieutenant-General Thomas Gage (1721–87), the last royal governor of Massachusetts (1774), to seize ammunition stored at Concord on April 19. It was not until November 9 that the colonies learned of the refusal of their petition to the king, who had declared them to be in a state of rebellion.

Franklin's dual role in England had raised doubts on both sides as to his true loyalty. Colonial radicals, on the one hand, had regarded him as pro-English; and the English, on the other hand, had looked upon him as a radical. After the Stamp Act and the Tea Act he had lost face and much good will at home, where he was not recognized as the anonymous author of the satirical articles *Rules by which a Great Empire May Be Reduced to a Small One* and *Edict by the King of Prussia*. In England, after a newspaper letter calling for American action, he was dubbed "Dr. Doubleface" and the "Judas of Craven Street". Nevertheless, he was truly a moderate until the time of the American Revolution. There was, however, no question as to his patriotism after his public disgrace.

The day following his arrival, Franklin was designated a Pennsylvania delegate to the Second Continental Congress (1775), its oldest member. He was made first Postmaster General of the Colonies. In July Franklin presented a paper to the Congress, as a committee of the whole, on suggested *Articles of Confederation and Perpetual Union*, which went beyond his 1754 proposal in espousing independence and national sovereignty. The Congress, however, was not yet ready—it did not even record the presentation. The following January a more provocative publication, *Common Sense*, appeared anonymously; it had been written by a bankrupt Englishman, Thomas Paine (1737–1809), who had been encouraged by Franklin to emigrate to Philadelphia in 1774. The matter came to a head on June 7, 1776, when the Virginian Richard Henry Lee (1732–94, later a senator) moved to implement the proposal for immediate independence. The committee appointed to prepare a suitable document consisted of John Adams (1735–1826, later President) of Massachusetts, Robert R. Livingston (1746–1813, later senator) of New York, Thomas Jefferson (1743–1826, later President) of Virginia, Roger Sherman (1721–93) of Connecticut, and Franklin. The resulting Declaration of Independence was adopted on July 4; the good news was pealed by the Liberty Bell (cast in England, 1752) in the State House (begun in 1732, now called Independence Hall).

Having served on a congressional committee which drafted a plan of 1776 for a model treaty of amity and commerce, Franklin was appointed a commissioner to negotiate such treaties in Europe, together with Silas Deane (1737–89), a Connecticut lawyer, and Jefferson, who declined and was replaced by Arthur Lee (1740–92), a Virginia lawyer. The other commissioners became involved in controversy, so that they were recalled in 1778 and 1779 respectively. Deane was replaced by Adams, who recommended that Franklin be appointed the single minister to France—a country that had been historically an enemy of England and Roman Catholic.

In the meantime, at the age of 70, when most men retire to seek a phantom of quiet and leisure, which Franklin had always envisaged for scientific investigations, suffering from the gout, he set out once more for Europe to play the role of a sincere politician dealing with factional policies at home and of a shrewd diplomat persuading cautious governments abroad. This next period turned out to be his "busiest and most brilliant decade in public service".

A representative portrait of Franklin during this period is the 1766 thumb one done by David Martin (1737–98); it was given to the White House during its recent (1962) refurbishing by Mrs. John Kennedy.

CHAPTER 4

American Sage

THE reception of Franklin in France was greater than that for any other American before or after him. Franklin, indeed, was the first American to attain a truly international reputation; his prestige as a natural philosopher was America's greatest asset abroad. He was more or less the official representative of its learning. His colleague John Adams, who differed with him on many fundamentals but who did not allow an underlying hostility to flare out until after the peace treaty, reported, somewhat exaggeratedly, that his reputation was "more universal than Leibniz [Baron Gottfried Wilhelm von (1664–1716), German philosopher and mathematician] or Newton [Sir Isaac (1642–1727), English natural philosopher and mathematician], Frederick [II the Great (1712–86), King of Prussia, patron of literature] or Voltaire [Francis Marie Arouet (1694–1778), French writer]." He shared in the philosophy of the age of enlightenment; he participated in the Académie Royale des Sciences; a highlight was his meeting there in 1778 with Voltaire. He associated with scientists—Buffon, Dalibard, and the chemist Antoine Laurent Lavoisier (1743–1794); — he had casual contacts with Jacobin revolutionists and the Incorruptible Maximelles François Marie Isidore de Robespierre (1758–94) about lightning rods in 1783, and Jean Paul Marat (1749–93) about fire in 1779. The French popularly regarded Franklin as a cross between the witty urbane Voltaire and the savage-loving Jean Jacques Rousseau (1712–78). (He was actually more like the former.) Franklin renewed his ties with the physiocrats, whose agricultural emphasis he endorsed; on visits from London in 1767 and 1769 he had met François Quesnay (1694–1774), economist and physician to Louis XV.

The finance minister and economist Anne Robert Jacques Turgot, Baron de l'Aulne (1727–81), in 1776 made the Latin epigram "Eripuit coelo fulmen sceptrumque tyrannis" (he snatched lightning from the sky and the scepter from the tyrant), which was used in the famous 1778 design by Jean Honoré Fragonard (1732–1806).

When Franklin landed in Brittany with William Temple (aged 16) and Benjamin Franklin Bache (aged 7) he wore his fur cap on account of the cold. (His choice of his incompetent grand son as secretary was unfortunate.) The people looked with amazement at this short, fat, wigless man wearing unfashionable spectacles as representative of an imagined primitive society. He seized upon their curiosity as an opportunity to play such a role with the cap as a symbol; his popularity contributed to the success of his mission. Donatien le Ray de Chaumont, a merchant and minor government official, offered him and Silas Deane comparatively secluded living quarters in the Hôtel de Valentinois in Passy (now the intersection of Rue Singer and Rue Raynouard) on a hill overlooking the Seine just outside Paris, beyond the fashionable Bois de Boulogne. Enjoying ease, he dined here biweekly with some neighbors; Abbé André Morellet (1727–1819), a contributor to the philosopher Denis Diderot's (1713–1784) Encyclopédie (1751–72), Abbé de la Roche, and the physiologist Jean Georges Cabanis (1757–1808). He was friendly also with the Mayor of Passy, Louis le Veillard (1733–94), and his wife. Another friend was the physicist Jean-Baptiste le Roy (1720–1800), who was in charge of the king's laboratory at La Muette in Passy.

Franklin was particularly intimate with some feminine neighbors who were charmed by his almost French gallantries and bons mots, and who, in turn, delighted him with their attentions and conversations. A close companion was the youthful and affectionate Mme Anne Louisa Boivin d'Hardancourt Brillon du Jouy (1744–1824), wife of a treasury official; she regarded him as a father and occasionally sat on his knee. Mme Catherine Helvétius was the wise and wealthy widow of the farmer-general and philosopher, Claude Adrien Helvétius (1715–71), a femme savante, friend of Voltaire and Turgot, who was wont to hold hands or put her arm about Franklin's neck at dinner;

he called her Notre Dame d'Auteuil (she rejected his proposal of marriage). He was acquainted also with the nearby Comtesse d'Houdetat, Rousseau's "Sophie". Franklin liked to converse with people; he himself would reminisce pleasantly and illustrate his points with moral tales. He would play chess 2–3 hours at a time (once from 6 p.m. until 6 a.m.); later in Philadelphia he had to resort to card playing. He was on good terms with the village priest and local tradesmen. His curiosity was boundless.

Franklin established a printing press at Passy (he invented a rolling press for copying letters), primarily to promote the public understanding of America. Even as late as 1784 he wrote two important tracts: *Information to Those Who Would come to America* and *Remarks Concerning the Savages of North America*. He could not, however, forbear making hoaxes. The French novelist Honoré de Balzac (1799–1850) remarked later that Franklin was the inventor of the lightning rod, the hoax, and the republic.

France became flooded with likenesses of Franklin: portraits and prints, busts and medallions, rings, and snuff boxes, etc. One of the best portraits is the so-called fur collar 1778 oil painting of the court painter Joseph Silfred Duplessis (1725–1802)—now at the New York Metropolitan Museum of Art. A good likeness during this period is the 1777 terra cotta bust (cover) by the sculptor Jean Jacques Caffiéri (1725–1792)—now at the Paris Bibliothèque Mazarine.

Louise XVI (1754–93) was then King of France; Franklin had met him when not yet 20, when he ascended the throne in 1774. The king, however, did not officially receive Franklin at Versailles until 1778. On the one hand, France, smarting from its defeat by the English in the French and Indian war, looked favorably on the American hostility to its arch-enemy; the people, too, were quite sympathetic to the colonial ideals of natural liberty and republican virtue. On the other hand, France was eager for the support of its Catholic ally Charles III (1716–88) of Spain, which looked enviously at Gibraltar (a secret agreement was made between the two countries in 1779—without the knowledge of America). The whole procedure was further complicated by the personal ambitions of the French courtier and dramatist

Pierre Augustin Caron de Beaumarchais (1732–99) and by the misguided actions of Franklin's colleagues, the naive Deane and the suspicious Lee. Fortunately, the French Minister of Foreign Affairs, Charles Gravier, Comte de Vergennes (1717–1787), had confidence in Franklin and secretly encouraged him; he, in turn, showed himself to be a shrewd diplomat. Despite American dissensions, the tide turned with news of the 1777 Saratoga defeat of the English commander (and dramatist) John Burgoyne (1722–92). At the subsequent signing of the amity and commerce treaty, Franklin proudly wore the Manchester velvet which he had on at the time of his Whitehall disgrace. In 1778 France granted a loan of 3 million livres; 4 years later it amounted to 18 million. The other commissioners were not successful in their dealings with Berlin, Florence, Madrid, St. Petersburg, and Vienna. Only Holland, at war with England in 1780, agreed to a treaty and loan on the eve of peace owing to the activity of a new (1781) Commissioner, Henry Laurens (1724–92), of South Carolina. In 1783 a treaty of amity and commerce was signed with Sweden. (Jefferson, also appointed a commissioner, did not arrive until 1784; subsequently he succeeded Franklin with whom he had much in common.)

Franklin, meanwhile, had multiple duties such as consul general, director of naval operations (privateers), judge of admiralty (prizes), and even arranged for the exchange of prisoners (e.g. Cornwallis and Jay). (Upon reaching the age of 75 he had offered to resign, but was requested by Congress to continue.) He had to recommend individuals desiring to go to America. Among these was M. J. P. Y. P. S. du Motier, Marquis de Lafayette (1757–1834), who offered to serve the Continental Army at 20, and the Prussian Baron F. W. L. S. Augustin von Steuben (1730–94)—both of whom became major-generals. The war came abruptly to an end with the 1781 surrender at Yorktown of Major-General Charles Cornwallis (1738–1805). In 1783 a peace treaty was signed by the commissioners John Jay (1745–1829), Adams, and Franklin. A week later he wrote to the Boston merchant Josiah Quincy (1710–84), "May we never see another war. For in my opinion there never was a good war or a bad peace."

Although Franklin never attained his retirement goal, viz. to return to scientific pursuits, he did find some leisure in Paris; Congress finally permitted him to return home in 1785. Unfortunately, he was greatly bothered by his gout, bladder stone, and failing eyesight. He did, however, join 50,000 people in watching the first ascent of a hydrogen-filled silk balloon sent up at the Camps-de-Mar by the French physicist Jacques Alexandre César Charles (1746–1823). The brother inventors Montgolfier, Joseph Michel (1740–1810) and Jacques Étienne (1745–99), had earlier made a heated-air balloon rise for 10 minutes at Ammonay, near Lyons. Later at Versailles they sent aloft a sheep, a cock, and a duck. Their first human passenger took flight from the Chateau de la Muette. That same year Charles and one other rose 2000 ft from the Tuileries; they landed safely 7 leagues from Paris. Franklin could not refrain from speculating on this new form of aerial navigation and its potential use for war. A similar demonstration was arranged in Philadelphia by the American Philosophical Society. An American loyalist was the first to fly across the English Channel.

A year later Paris (including Lafayette) was captivated by the fad of "animal magnetism" promulgated by the Austrian physician Friedrich Anton Mesmer (1734–1815), whose work had been repudiated at Vienna and Berlin. His claim to cure diseases was investigated by a royal commission from the Académie Royale des Sciences, which included the physician Joseph Ignace Guillotin (1738–1844), Lavoisier, Franklin, and others. Some of the tests were actually performed at Franklin's house at Passy. Their report exposed some of the charlatanry and denied the experimental existence of any such phenomenon.

On September 14 Franklin again landed at the Market St. Wharf, this time with 128 boxes amid the joyful ringing of bells and the impressive roaring of cannon. On the return voyage he had written more scientific articles than during any other comparable period in his life. That Fall he was elected in short order to the Council, to its presidency, and to the presidency of Pennsylvania (by joint action with the Assembly). In 1787 he became president of a new Society for Political Enquiries, supposed to be comparable to the American Philosophical Society for natural sciences. He was chosen a delegate to the Constitutional Convention—its oldest member. He served on a critical committee for resolving the dispute between those wishing representation by equal states and those demanding population consideration. He suggested a compromise, the present bicameral Congress, which has a group based upon each principle. This committee's recommendation, coupled with Franklin's realistic presentation, a masterpiece for unity, resulted in adoption by the Convention on September 17—now called Constitution Day. He had slyly remarked with reference to the picture behind Washington's chair that painters never distinguished a setting sun and a rising sun.

Pennsylvania adopted the Constitution in December at a special convention. On September 16, 1788, the last requisite colony had ratified it. On that very day Franklin resigned his presidency—the last act of his political career—at age 82.

Meanwhile, he had become interested in real estate. In 1787 he had built three houses and was planning two more. He had added an addition to his own, a dining room to seat twenty-four, with a library above it, two lodging rooms above that, and an attic on top.

He had become President of the Pennsylvania Society for Promoting Abolition of Slavery, founded by the Quakers in 1775—the first of its kind. In February 1790 he signed a memorial and submitted it to Congress—the last act of his public service—at age 84.

After a long, painful illness, he died on April 17. Four days later a *cortège* of some 20,000, including the physician Benjamin Rush (*C.* 1745–1813) and the astronomer and first Director of the United States Mint, David Rittenhouse (1732–96), who succeeded him as President of the American Philosophical Society, proceeded from the State House to the Christ Church burial ground; it comprised representatives of his many interests. There he was laid to rest, believing in the immortality of the soul and justice in the life to come.

A eulogy was given before the Académie Royale des Sciences by the philosopher and Girondist M. J. A. Nicholas de Caritat, Marquis de Condorcet (1743–94); the National Assembly of France, on motion by the Jacobin, H. G. V. Riquiti, Comte de Mirabeau (1749–91), went into mourning for three days. The clergyman and educator William Smith (1727–1803), a long-time personal enemy of Franklin, was selected to give a eulogy before the American Philosophical Society; the House of Representatives had a month period of mourning; the Senate had none.

His last will had been carefully drawn up in 1788 for all to witness; it crystallized his remembrances of gratitude and of opposition; he manumitted his personal slave Bob; he reprimanded his disloyal son William. It included a famous codicil of progressive philanthropy for Boston and for Philadelphia. These trust funds have continued to grow; by the year 2000 the Boston fund will amount to more than $2,000,000.

Our Franklin heritage, however, is not to be measured by his possessions or even by his achievements—great though they are—but rather by his life as a wholesome person who touched with a healing heart and hand people of all ages in all walks of life. He himself, however, was always the same; he had personal integrity.

Chronology

1706	Born January 17 (NS) in Boston, Massachusetts.
1714	Attends school.
1716	Assists father in soap and candle business.
1718	Apprenticed to brother James, a printer.
1722	Writes Silence Dogood papers.
1723	Runs away to Philadelphia, Pennsylvania; works in printing shop.
1725	Sails to England; works in printing shops.
1726	Returns to Philadelphia; works in store and printing shop.
1727	Organizes Junto.
1728	Opens own printing shop (Meredith partner).
1729	Publishes the *Pennsylvania Gazette*.
1730	Appointed printer to the Assembly.
	Dissolves Meredith partnership.
	"Marries" Deborah Read.
1731	Son, William Franklin (illegitimate), born.
	Organizes Library Co.
1732	Son, Francis Folger, Franklin, born.
	Publishes first (1753) *Poor Richard: An Almanack*.
1736	Francis Folger Franklin dies.
	Appointed Assembly clerk.
	Organizes Union Fire Co.
1737	Appointed Philadelphia postmaster.
1739–40	Invents Pennsylvania fireplace.
1743	Publishes *Proposal for Promoting Useful Knowledge*.
	Daughter, Sarah Franklin born.

1747   Begins electric experiments.

Organizes Association for Pennsylvania defense.

1748   Forms printing partnership with David Hall, retires from active service.

Elected member of Philadelphia Common Council.

1749   Elected president of trustees of Academy of Philadelphia.

1751   *Experiments and Observations on Electricity* book published.

Elected Philadelphia member of Assembly.

Elected Philadelphia alderman.

1752   Organizes Fire Insurance Co.

Franklin experiment performed in Europe.

Performs kite experiment in Philadelphia.

1753   Awarded honorary MA by Harvard and by Yale.

Awarded Copley Medal of Royal Society of London.

Appointed deputy postmaster general of North America (with William Hunter).

Part II of book published.

1754   Proposes Plan of Union at Albany Congress.

Part III of book published.

1755   Assists General Braddock in procuring transportation.

Elected president of managers of Pennsylvania Hospital.

Assists in organizing defense against Indians.

1756   Awarded honorary MA by William and Mary.

Elected Fellow of the Royal Society.

Organizes Philadelphia militia.

1757   Sails to England as Assembly agent.

Publishes *The Way to Wealth* as preface to *Poor Richard* (1758).

1759   Awarded honorary LL D degree by University of St. Andrews, Scotland.

Elected member of Royal Society Council.

1762   Awarded honorary DCL by Oxford University.

Describes armonica.

Returns to Philadelphia.

1763   Builds new house.

1764   Elected Assembly speaker, then defeated for membership.
       Returns to England as Assembly agent.
1765   Stamp Act passed.
       Elected member of Royal Society Council.
1766   Writes anonymously in London newspapers against Stamp
           Act; examined by House of Commons.
       Stamp Act repealed.
       Printing partnership with Hall expires.
       Elected member of Royal Society Council.
1767   Townshend Duty Act passed.
       Visits Paris with Pringle.
       Sarah Franklin marries Richard Bache.
1768   Appointed agent for Georgia province.
1769   Elected president of American Philosophical Society (annu-
           ally for life).
       Visits France.
       Appointed agent of New Jersey House of Representatives.
1770   Townshend duties repealed (except tea).
       Appointed agent of Massachusetts House of Representa-
           tives.
1771   Writes Part I of *Autobiography* at Twyford.
1772   Elected member of Royal Society Council.
       Elected corresponding member of French Académie Royale
           des Sciences.
1773   Tea Act passed; Boston Tea Party.
1774   Attacked for role in Hutchinson letters by Solicitor General be-
           fore Privy Council Committee on Massachusetts petition.
       Dismissed as deputy postmaster general.
       Deborah Read Franklin dies.
1775   Returns to Philadelphia.
       Selected as Pennsylvania delegate to Second Continental
           Congress.
       Elected postmaster general by Congress.
1776   Member of committee to draft Declaration of Independence,
           adopted July 4, 1776.

Elected Pennsylvania delegate to Constitutional Convention. Appointed one of three commissioners to French court; arrives in Paris.

1777   Surrender of Burgoyne at Saratoga.

1778   Treaty of alliance and of amity and commerce with France, loan; received by Louis XVI.

1779   Appointed sole minister plenipotentiary at French Court.

1781   Surrender of Cornwallis at Yorktown.

1783   Peace Treaty.

Writes Part II of *Autobiography*.

1785   Returns to Philadelphia.

Elected member of Pennsylvania Supreme Executive Council; then president (3 years).

1786   Enlarges house.

1787   Organizes Society for Political Enquiries; elected president.

Elected president of Pennsylvania Society for Promoting the Abolition of Slavery.

Made a Pennsylvania delegate to Federal Constitutional Convention; moves in Committee the "Great Compromise" on representation; makes closing Convention Speech.

1788   Makes last will and testament, with codicil.

Begins Part III of *Autobiography*.

1790   Dies April 17; buried on April 21 in Christ Church burial ground.

PART II
HIS SCIENTIFIC LETTERS

CHAPTER 5

Hot and Cold

(a) Thermal Conduction and Evaporation

For centuries the only thermometers were human beings. Despite their familiarity with the feeling of hot and cold, they did not understand the nature of heat until the nineteenth century. Franklin cites many familiar phenomena. Based upon the experience that when one end of a metal rod is heated the other end will gradually become warm, too, man early thought of heat as some kind of material that would flow from hot to cold like water flows down hill. (The term caloric was introduced in 1789 by the French chemist Lavoisier.) One spoke of good conductors of heat and poor conductors or insulators. Franklin himself noted that good electric conductors are also good thermal conductors.

Nowadays one interprets such phenomena on the basis of the kinetic theory of matter; temperature is regarded theoretically as the average kinetic energy of atoms. (The kinetic energy in this instance is one-half the mass of an atom times its speed squared.) Atoms with higher average kinetic energy will transmit some of it to their neighbors upon impact. It is amazing that it took man so long to measure temperature objectively.

The first thermoscope was devised in 1606 by the Italian founder of modern physics, Galileo Galilei (1564–1642); it was merely a detector of change. By the end of the seventeenth century quantitative thermometers had been developed by using fixed-point (one or two) methods of calibration. The first air thermometer independent of barometric pressure was developed in 1702 by the French physicist

Guillaume Amontons (1663–1705). It stimulated the German instrument-maker Gabriel Daniel Fahrenheit (1686–1736) to produce convenient, accurate thermometers containing mercury. It is surprising to note the number of such thermometers sent from England by Franklin to colonial scientists. In 1731 René Antoine Ferchault, Seigneur Réaumur, des Angles et de la Bermodière (1683–1757), independently developed a thermometer with spirit of wine (one-fifth water) and a different scale. The thermometers themselves were not well constructed, so that comparable readings were difficult. The Centigrade scale with its convenient 100 degrees between the two fixed points has become quite common. An international temperature scale was defined in 1927 by a series of fixed points determined by gas-thermometer measurements.

Evaporation takes place when the faster moving atoms escape from any material, thus lowering the average kinetic energy of those atoms remaining, i.e. the temperature. In 1768 Franklin mentioned the so-called pulse glass, which he had seen in Germany.

To JOHN LINING. *April 14, 1757*

It is a long time since I had the pleasure of a line from you; and, indeed, the troubles of our country, with the hurry of business I have been engaged in on that account, have made me so bad a correspondent, that I ought not to expect punctuality in others.

But, being about to embark for England, I could not quit the continent without paying my respects to you, and, at the same time, taking leave to introduce to your acquaintance a gentleman of learning and merit, Colonel Henry Bouquet, who does me the favour to present you this letter, and with whom I am sure you will be much pleased.

Professor Simson, of Glasgow, lately communicated to me some curious experiments of a physician of his acquaintance, by which it appeared that an extraordinary degree of cold, even to freezing, might be produced by evaporation. I have not had leisure to repeat and

examine more than the first and easiest of them, viz. Wet the ball of
a thermometer by a feather dipped in spirit of wine, which has been
kept in the same room, and has, of course, the same degree of heat
or cold. The mercury sinks presently three or four degrees, and the
quicker, if, during the evaporation, you blow on the ball with bellows;
a second wetting and blowing, when the mercury is down, carries it
yet lower. I think I did not get it lower than five or six degrees from
where it naturally stood, which was, at that time, sixty. But it is said,
that a vessel of water being placed in another somewhat larger, containing spirit, in such a manner that the vessel of water is surrounded
with the spirit, and both placed under the receiver of an air-pump;
on exhausting the air, the spirit, evaporating, leaves such a degree
of cold as to freeze the water, though the thermometer, in the open
air, stands many degrees above the freezing point.

I known not how this phenomenon is to be accounted for; but it
gives me occasion to mention some loose notions relating to heat and
cold, which I have for some time entertained, but not yet reduced into
any form. Allowing common fire, as well as electrical, to be a fluid
capable of permeating other bodies, and seeking an equilibrium, I
imagine some bodies are better fitted by nature to be conductors of
that fluid than others; and that, generally, those which are the best
conductors of the electrical fluid, are also the best conductors of this;
and e contra.

Thus a body which is a good conductor of fire readily receives it into
its substance, and conducts it through the whole to all the parts, as
metals and water do; and if two bodies, both good conductors, one
heated, the other in its common state, are brought into contact with
each other, the body which has most fire readily communicates of it
to that which had least, and that which had least readily receives it,
till an equilibrium is produced. Thus, if you take a dollar between
your fingers with one hand, and a piece of wood, of the same dimensions, with the other, and bring both at the same time to the flame
of a candle, you will find yourself obliged to drop the dollar before
you drop the wood, because it conducts the heat of the candle sooner
to your flesh. Thus, if a silver tea-pot had a handle of the same metal,

it would conduct the heat from the water to the hand, and become too hot to be used; we therefore give to a metal tea-pot a handle of wood, which is not so good a conductor as metal. But a china or stone tea-pot being in some degree of the nature of glass, which is not a good conductor of heat, may have a handle of the same stuff. Thus, also, a damp moist air shall make a man more sensible of cold, or chill him more, than a dry air that is colder, because a moist air is fitter to receive and conduct away the heat of his body. This fluid, entering bodies in great quantity first expands them by separating their parts a little, afterwards, by farther separating their parts, it renders solids fluid, and at length dissipates their parts in air. Take this fluid from melted lead, or from water, the parts cohere again; (the first grows solid, the latter becomes ice;) and this is sooner done by the means of good conductors. Thus, if you take, as I have done, a square bar of lead, four inches long, and one inch thick, together with three pieces of wood planed to the same dimensions, and lay them, as in the margin, on a smooth board, fixed so as not to be easily separated or moved, and pour into the cavity they form, as much melted lead as will fill it, you will see the melted lead chill, and become firm, on the side next the leaden bar, some time before it chills on the other three sides in contact with the wooden bars, though, before the lead was poured in, they might all be supposed to have the same degree of heat or coldness, as they had been exposed in the same room to the same air. You will likewise observe, that the leaden bar, as it has cooled the melted lead more than the wooden bars have done, so it is itself more heated by the melted lead. There is a certain quantity of this fluid, called fire, in every living human body, which fluid, being in due proportion, keeps the parts of the flesh and blood at such a just distance from each other, as that the flesh and nerves are supple, and the blood fit for circulation. If part of this due proportion of fire be conducted away, by means of a contact with other bodies, as air, water, or metals, the parts of our skin and flesh that come into such contact first draw more near together than is agreeable, and give that sensation which we call cold; and if too much be conveyed away, the body stiffens, the blood ceases to flow, and death ensues. On the other hand, if too much of this fluid be communicated to the flesh, the parts are separated too far, and pain ensues, as when they are separated by a pin or lancet. The sensation, that the separation by fire occasions, we call heat, or burning. My desk on which I now write, and the lock of my desk, are both exposed to the same temperature of the air, and have therefore the same degree of heat or cold; yet if I lay my hand successively

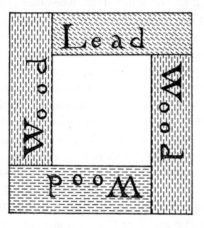

on the wood and on the metal, the latter feels much the coldest, not that it is really so, but, being a better conductor, it more readily than the wood takes away and draws into itself the fire that was in my skin. Accordingly if I lay one hand, part on the lock, and part on the wood, and, after it has lain so some time, I feel both Parts with my other Hand, I find that Part that has been in Contact with the Lock, very sensibly colder to the Touch, than the Part that lay on the Wood. How a living Animal obtains its Quantity of this Fluid, called Fire, is a curious Question. I have shewn, that some Bodies (as Metals) have a Power of attracting it stronger than others; and I have sometimes suspected, that a living Body had some Power of attracting out of the Air, or other Bodies, the Heat it wanted. Thus Metals hammered, or repeatedly bent grow hot in the bent or hammer'd part. But when I consider that Air, in Contact with the Body, cools it; that the surrounding Air is rather heated by its Contact with the Body; that every breath of cooler Air, drawn in, carries off Part of the Body's Heat when it passes out again; that therefore there must be some Fund in the Body for producing it, or otherwise the Animal would soon grow cold; I have been rather inclined to think, that the Fluid *Fire*, as well as the Fluid *Air*, is attracted by Plants in their Growth, and becomes consolidated with the other Materials of which they are formed, and makes a great Part of their Substance. That, when they come to be digested, and to suffer in the Vessels a kind of Fermentation, part of the Fire, as well as part of the Air, recovers its fluid, active State again, and diffuses itself in the Body digesting and separating it. That the Fire, so reproduced by Digestion and Separation, continually leaving the Body, its Place is supplied by fresh Quantities, arising from the continual Separation. That whatever quickens the Motion of the Fluids in an Animal quickens the Separation, and reproduces more of the Fire as Exercise. That all the Fire emitted by Wood and other Combustibles when burning existed in them before in a solid State, being only discover'd when separating. That some Fossils, as Sulphur, Sea-Coal, &c., contain a great deal of solid Fire. And that in short, what escapes and is dissipated in the burning of Bodies, besides Water and Earth, is generally the Air and Fire that before made Parts of the Solid. Thus I imagine, that Animal Heat arises by or from a kind of Fermentation in the Juices of the Body, in the same manner as Heat arises in the Liquors preparing for Distillation, wherein there is a Separation of the Spirituous, from the Watery and Earthy Parts. And it is remarkable, that the Liquor in a Distiller's Vat, when in its highest and best State of Fermentation, as I have been inform'd, has the same Degree of Heat with the Human Body, that is about 94 or 96.

Thus, as by a constant supply of Fuel in a Chimney, you keep a warm Room, so, by a constant supply of Food in the Stomach, you keep a warm Body; only where little Exercise is used, the Heat may possibly be conducted away too fast; in which Case such Materials are to be used for Cloathing and Bedding, against the Effects of an immediate contact of the Air, as are, in themselves, bad Conductors of Heat, and, consequently prevent its being communicated thro' their Substances to the Air. Hence what is called *Warmth* in Wool, and its Preference, on that Account, to Linnen; Wool not being so good a Conductor. And hence all the natural Coverings of Animals, to keep them warm, are such as retain and confine the natural Heat in the Body by being bad Conductors, such as Wool, Hair, Feathers, and the Silk by which the Silk-Worm, in its tender embrio State, is first cloathed. Cloathing thus considered does not make a Man warm by *giving* Warmth, but by *preventing* the too quick dissipation of the Heat produced in his Body, and so occasioning an Accumulation.

There is another curious Question I will just venture to touch upon, viz. Whence arises the sudden extraordinary Degree of Cold, perceptible on mixing some chymical Liquors, and even on mixing Salt and Snow, where the Composition appears colder than the coldest of the Ingredients? I have never seen the chymical Mixtures made; but Salt and Snow I have often mixed myself, and am fully satisfied that the Composition feels much colder to the Touch, and lowers the Mercury in the Thermometer more, than either Ingredient would do separately. I suppose, with others, that Cold is nothing more than the Absence of Heat or Fire. Now if the Quantity of Fire before contained or diffused in the Snow and Salt was expell'd in the uniting of the two Matters, it must be driven away either thro' the Air or the Vessel containing them. If it is driven off thro' the Air, it must warm the Air; and a Thermometer held over the Mixture, without touching it, would discover the Heat, by the rising of the Mercury, as it must, and always does, in warmer Air.

This indeed I have not try'd but I should guess it would rather be driven off thro' the Vessel, especially if the Vessel be Metal, as being a better Conductor than Air, and so one should find the Bason warmer after such Mixture. But on the Contrary the Vessel grows cold, and even Water, in which the Vessel is sometimes placed for the Experiment, freezes into hard Ice on the Bason. Now I know not how to account for this, otherwise than by supposing, that the Composition is a better Conductor of Fire than the Ingredients separately and like the Lock compar'd with the Wood, has a stronger Power of Attracting Fire, and does accordingly attract it suddenly from the Fingers, or a Thermometer put into it, from the Bason that contains it, and from the Water in Contact with the outside of the Bason; so that the Fingers have the Sensation of extreme Cold, by being depriv'd of much of their natural Fire; the Thermometer sinks, by having part of its Fire drawn out of the Mercury; the Bason grows colder to the Touch, as by having its Fire drawn into the Mixture, it is become more capable of drawing and receiving it from the Hand, and thro' the Bason, the Water loses its Fire that kept it fluid; so it becomes Ice. One would expect, that from all this attracted Acquisition of Fire to the Composition, it should become warmer; and, in Fact, the Snow and Salt dissolve at the same time into Water, without freezing.

I doubt whether I have in all this talk'd intelligibly; and indeed how should a Man do so that does not himself clearly understand the Thing he talks of? This I confess to be my present Case. I intended to amuse you, but I fear I have done more and tired you. Be so good as to excuse it.

B. FRANKLIN

To JOHN LINING. *June 17, 1758*

In a former letter I mentioned the experiment for cooling bodies by evaporation, and that I had, by repeatedly wetting the thermometer with common spirits, brought the mercury down five or six degrees. Being lately at *Cambridge*, and mentioning this in conversation with Dr. *Hadley*, professor of chemistry there, he proposed repeating the experiments with ether, instead of common spirits, as the ether is much quicker in evaporation. We accordingly went to his chamber, where he had both ether and a thermometer. By dipping first the ball of the thermometer into the ether, it appeared that the ether was precisely of the same temperament with the thermometer, which stood then at 65; for it made no alteration in the height of the little column of mercury. But when the thermometer was taken out of the ether, and the ether, with which the ball was wet, began to evaporate, the mercury sunk several degrees. The wetting was then repeated by a feather that had been dipped into the ether, when the mercury sunk still lower.

We continued this operation, one of us wetting the ball, and another of the company blowing on it with the bellows, to quicken the evaporation, the mercury sinking all the time, till it came down to 7, which is 25 degrees below the freezing point, when we left off. Soon after it passed the freezing point, a thin coat of ice began to cover the ball. Whether this was water collected and condensed by the coldness of the ball, from the moisture in the air, or from our breath; or whether the feather, when dipped into the ether, might not sometimes go through it, and bring up some of the water that was under it, I am not certain; perhaps all might contribute. The ice continued increasing till we ended the experiment, when it appeared near a quarter of an inch thick all over the ball, with a number of small *spicula*, pointing outwards. From this experiment one may see the possibility of freezing a man to death on a warm summer's day, if he were to stand in a passage through which the wind blew briskly, and to be wet frequently with ether, a spirit that is more inflammable than brandy, or common spirits of wine.

It is but within these few years, that the *European* philosophers seem to have known this power in nature, of cooling bodies by evaporation. But in the east they have long been acquainted with it. A friend tells me, there is a passage in *Bernier's* Travels through *Indostan,* written near one hundred years ago, that mentions it as a practice (in traveling over dry desarts in that hot climate) to carry water in flasks wrapt in wet woollen cloths, and hung on the shady side of the camel, or carriage, but in the free air; whereby, as the cloths gradually grow drier, the water contained in the flasks is made cool. They have likewise a kind of earthen pots, unglaz'd, which let the water gradually and slowly ooze through their pores, so as to keep the outside a little wet, notwithstanding the continual evaporation, which gives great coldness to the vessel, and the water contained in it. Even our common sailors seem to have had some notion of this property; for I remember, that being at sea, when I was a youth, I observed one of the sailors, during a calm in the night, often wetting his finger in his mouth, and then holding it up in the air, to discover, as he said, if the air had any motion, and from which side it came; and this he expected to do, by finding one side of his finger grow suddenly cold, and from that side he should look for the next wind; which I then laughed at as a fancy.

May not several phænomena, hitherto unconsidered, or unaccounted for, be explained by this property? During the hot *Sunday* at *Philadelphia*, in *June* 1750, when the thermometer was up at 100 in the shade, I sat in my chamber without exercise, only reading or writing, with no other cloaths on than a shirt, and a pair of long linen drawers, the windows all open, and a brisk wind blowing through the house; the sweat ran off the backs of my hands, and my shirt was often so wet, as to induce me to call for dry ones to put on. In this situation, one might have expected, that the natural heat of the body 96, added to the heat of the air 100, should jointly have created or produced a much greater degree of heat in the body; but the fact was, that my body never grew so hot as the air that surrounded it, or the inanimate bodies immersed in the same air. For I remember well, that the desk, when I laid my arm upon it; a chair, when I sat down in it; and a dry shirt out of the drawer, when I put it on, all felt exceeding warm to me, as if they had been warmed before a fire. And I suppose a dead body would have acquired the temperature of the air, though a living one, by continual sweating, and by the evaporation of that sweat, was kept cold.

May not this be a reason why our reapers in *Pensylvania*, working in the open field in the clear hot sunshine common in our harvest-time,[1] find themselves well able to go through that labour, without being much incommoded by the heat, while they continue to sweat, and while they supply matter for keeping up that sweat, by drinking frequently of a thin evaporable liquor, water mixed with rum; but, if the sweat stops, they drop, and sometimes die suddenly, if a sweating is not again brought on by drinking that liquor, or, as some rather chuse in that case, a kind of hot punch, made with water, mixed with honey, and a considerable proportion of vinegar? May there not

---

[1] *Pennsylvania* is in about lat. 40, and the sun, of course, about 12 degrees higher, and therefore much hotter, than in *England*. Their harvest is about the end of *June*, or beginning of *July*, when the sun is nearly at the highest.

be in negroes a quicker evaporation of the perspirable matter from their skins and lungs, which, by cooling them more, enables them to bear the sun's heat better than whites do? (if that is a fact, as it is said to be; for the alledg'd necessity of having negroes rather than whites, to work in the *West India* fields, is founded upon it) though the colour of their skins would otherwise make them more sensible of the sun's heat, since black cloth heats much sooner, and more, in the sun, than white cloth. I am persuaded, from several instances happening within my knowledge, that they do not bear cold weather so well as the whites; they will perish when exposed to a less degree of it, and are more apt to have their limbs frost-bitten; and may not this be from the same cause?

Would not the earth grow much hotter under the summer sun, if a constant evaporation from its surface, greater as the sun shines stronger, did not, by tending to cool it, balance, in some degree, the warmer effects of the sun's rays? Is it not owing to the constant evaporation from the surface of every leaf, that trees, though shone on by the sun, are always, even the leaves themselves, cool to our sense? at least, much cooler than they would otherwise be? May it not be owing to this, that fanning ourselves when warm, does really cool us, though the air is itself warm that we drive with the fan upon our faces? For the atmosphere round, and next to our bodies, having imbibed as much of the perspired vapour as it can well contain, receives no more, and the evaporation is therefore check'd and retarded, till we drive away that atmosphere, and bring dryer air in its place, that will receive the vapour, and thereby facilitate and increase the evaporation? Certain it is, that mere blowing of air on a dry body does not cool it, as any one may satisfy himself, by blowing with a bellows on the dry ball of a thermometer; the mercury will not fall; if it moves at all, it rather rises, as being warmed by the friction of the air on its surface.

To these queries of imagination, I will only add one practical observation; that wherever it is thought proper to give ease, in cases of painful inflammation in the flesh (as from burnings, or the like), by cooling the part; linen cloths wet with spirit, and applied to the part inflamed, will produce the coolness required, better than if wet with water, and will continue it longer. For water, though cold when first applied, will soon acquire warmth from the flesh, as it does not evaporate fast enough; but the cloths wet with spirit, will continue cold as long as any spirit is left to keep up the evaporation, the parts warmed escaping as soon as they are warmed, and carrying off the heat with them.

(b) Radiation and Thermal Absorption

Franklin was undoubtedly familiar with the Dutch physician Boerhaave's textbook on *Elementa Chemiae* (1832), which turned out to be a chemistry classic. In it he noted that the black portion of a cloth dried more quickly than the white part—presumably the origin of Franklin's own experiment with differently colored patches of cloth on snow. His conclusion that dark colors are better absorbers would be strictly true only if solar radiation were limited to rays in the visible spectrum. Even at moderate temperatures, however, any body gives out radiation of all wavelengths. In 1800 the astronomer Sir William Herschel (1738–1822) had detected rays beyond the red end of the spectrum, i.e. so-called infrared rays, with less energy so that they are more readily absorbed by molecules. Their thermal energy is then incorporated in the body's internal energy. Materials, however, have different degrees of diathermancy for these heat rays just as they do different transparency for light rays. The physicist John Tyndall (1820–93), successor to the physicist and chemist Michael Faraday (1791–1867), as Professor of Natural Philosophy in the Royal Institution, performed a critical demonstration there in his 1862 series of popular lectures on "*Heat considered as mode of motion*" (1866). He showed that a thermometer with its bulb coated with alum (a white powder) rose almost twice as high as a thermometer with its bulb covered with iodine (a dark powder). The phenomenon is more complex than Franklin naively supposed.

To MARY STEVENSON. *September 20, 1761*

As to our other Subject, the different Degrees of Heat imbibed from the Sun's Rays by Cloths of different Colours, since I cannot find the Notes of my Experiment to send you, I must give it as well as I can from Memory.

But first let me mention an Experiment you may easily make yourself. Walk but a quarter of an Hour in your Garden when the Sun shines, with a part of your Dress white, and a Part black; then apply your Hand to them alternately, and you will find a very great Difference in their Warmth. The Black will be quite hot to the Touch, the White still cool.

Another. Try to fire Paper with a burning Glass. If it is White, you will not easily burn it; but if you bring the Focus to a black Spot, or upon Letters, written or printed, the Paper will immediately be on fire under the Letters.

Thus Fullers and Dyers find black Cloths, of equal Thickness with white ones, and hung out equally wet, dry in the Sun much sooner than the white, being more readily heated by the Sun's Rays. It is the same before a Fire; the Heat of which sooner penetrates black Stockings than white ones, and so is apt sooner to burn a Man's Shins. Also Beer much sooner warms in a black Mug set before the Fire, than in a white-one, or in a bright Silver Tankard.

My Experiment was this. I took a number of little square Pieces of Broad Cloth from a Taylor's Pattern-Card, of various Colours. There were Black, deep Blue, lighter Blue, Green, Purple, Red, Yellow, White, and other Colours, or Shades of Colours. I laid them all out upon the Snow in a bright Sunshiny Morning. In a few Hours (I cannot now be exact as to the Time), the Black, being warm'd most by the Sun, was sunk so low as to be below the Stroke of the Sun's Rays; the dark Blue almost as low, the lighter Blue not quite so much as the dark, the other Colours less as they were lighter; and the quite White remain'd on the Surface of the Snow, not having entred it at all.

What signifies Philosophy that does not apply to some Use? May we not learn from hence, that black Clothes are not so fit to wear in a hot Sunny Climate or Season, as white ones; because in such Cloaths the Body is more heated by the Sun when we walk abroad, and are at the same time heated by the Exercise, which double Heat is apt to bring on putrid dangerous Fevers? That Soldiers and Seamen, who must march and labour in the Sun, should in the East or West Indies have an Uniform of white? That Summer Hats, for Men or Women, should be white, as repelling that Heat which gives Headachs to many, and to some the fatal Stroke that the French call the *Coup de Soleil?* That the Ladies' Summer Hats, however, should be lined with Black, as not reverberating on their Faces those Rays which are reflected upwards from the Earth or Water? That the putting a white Cap of Paper or Linnen *within* the Crown of a black Hat, as some do, will not keep out the Heat, tho' it would if placed *without?* That Fruit-Walls being black'd may receive so much Heat from the Sun in the Daytime, as to continue warm in some degree thro' the Night, and thereby preserve the Fruit from Frosts, or forward its Growth?—with sundry other particulars of less or greater Importance, that will occur from time to time to attentive Minds?

B. Franklin

CHAPTER 6

Water Ways

(a) Oil on Water

Whenever a liquid drop is formed, its surface seems to act like a stretched elastic bag. There is said to be a "surface tension" (term introduced by Johann Andreas von Segner in 1751) owing to the unbalanced force on surface molecules by their underlying neighbors (explanation about 1800). A slight film of grease produces a great decrease in the surface tension of water, inasmuch as grease molecules have much less attraction for water molecules, and by their very presence prevent normal attraction between neighboring water molecules.

Water waves can be calmed to some extent when oil is poured on them. The wind pushes the oil away, leaving behind pure water, which pulls back the weak, wind-disturbed water. In the case of existing waves, a variation of oil thickness is associated necessarily with differences in surface tension, thus destroying the regularity of the wave pattern. It should be noted that some oils, e.g. paraffin, do not spread at all on water.

William Brownrigg (1711–1800) was an English physician and chemist (FRS 1741) in Cumberland.

To JOHN PRINGLE. *December 1, 1762*

During our passage to Madeira, the weather being warm, and the cabbin windows constantly open for the benefit of the air, the candles at night flared and run very much, which was an inconvenience. At

53

Madeira we got oil to burn, and with a common glass tumbler or beaker, slung in wire, and suspended to the cieling of the cabbin, and a little wire hoop for the wick, furnish'd with corks to float on the oil, I made an Italian lamp, that gave us very good light all over the table. The glass at bottom contained water to about one third of its height; another third was taken up with oil; the rest was left empty that the sides of the glass might protect the flame from the wind. There is nothing remarkable in all this; but what follows is particular. At supper, looking on the lamp, I remarked that tho' the surface of the oil was perfectly tranquil, and duly preserved its position and distance with regard to the brim of the glass, the water under the oil was in great commotion, rising and falling in irregular waves, which continued during the whole evening. The lamp was kept burning as a watch-light all night, till the oil was spent, and the water only remain'd. In the morning I observed, that though the motion of the ship continued the same, the water was now quiet, and its surface as tranquil as that of the oil had been the evening before. At night again, when oil was put upon it, the water resum'd its irregular motions, rising in high waves almost to the surface of the oil, but without disturbing the smooth level of that surface. And this was repeated every day during the voyage.

Since my arrival in America, I have repeated the experiment frequently thus. I have put a pack-thread round a tumbler, with strings of the same, from each side, meeting above it in a knot at about a foot distance from the top of the tumbler. Then putting in as much water as would fill about one third part of the tumbler, I lifted it up by the knot, and swung it to and fro in the air; when the water appeared to keep its place in the tumbler as steadily as if it had been ice. But pouring gently in upon the water about as much oil, and then again swinging it in the air as before, the tranquility before possessed by the water was transferred to the surface of the oil, and the water under it was agitated with the same commotions as at sea.

I have shewn this experiment to a number of ingenious persons. Those who are but slightly acquainted with the principles of hydrostatics, &c. are apt to fancy immediately that they understand it, and readily attempt to explain it; but their explanations have been different, and to me not very intelligible. Others more deeply skilled in those principles, seem to wonder at it, and promise to consider it. And I think it is worth considering: For a new appearance, if it cannot be explain'd by our old principles, may afford us new ones, of use perhaps in explaining some other obscure parts of natural knowledge.

To WILLIAM BROWNRIGG. *November 7, 1773*

I thank you for the remarks of your learned friend at Carlisle. I had, when a youth, read and smiled at Pliny's account of a practice among the seamen of his time, to still the waves in a storm by pouring oil into the sea; which he mentions, as well as the use made of oil by the divers; but the stilling a tempest by throwing vinegar into the air had escaped me. I think with your friend, that it has been of late too much the mode to slight the learning of the ancients. The learned, too, are apt to slight too much the knowledge of the vulgar. The cooling by evaporation was long an instance of the latter. This art of smoothing the waves by oil is an instance of both.

Perhaps you may not dislike to have an account of all I have heard, and learnt, and done in this way. Take it if you please as follows.

In 1757, being at sea in a fleet of ninety-six sail bound against Louisbourg, I observed the wakes of two of the ships to be remarkably smooth, while all the others were ruffled by the wind, which blew fresh. Being puzzled with the differing appearance, I at last pointed it out to our captain, and asked him the meaning of it. "The cooks", says he, "have, I suppose, been just emptying their greasy water through the scuppers, which has greased the sides of those ships a little;" and this answer he gave me with an air of some little contempt, as to a person ignorant of what everybody else knew. In my own mind I at first slighted his solution, though I was not able to think of another; but recollecting what I had formerly read in Pliny, I resolved to make some experiment of the effect of oil on water, when I should have opportunity.

Afterwards being again at sea in 1762, I first observed the wonderful quietness of oil on agitated water, in the swinging glass lamp I made to hang up in the cabin, as described in my printed papers. This I was continually looking at and considering, as an appearance to me inexplicable. An old sea captain, then a passenger with me, thought little of it, supposing it an effect of the same kind with that of oil put on water to smooth it, which he said was a practice of the Bermudians when they would strike fish, which they could not see, if the surface of the water was ruffled by the wind. This practice I had never before heard of, and was obliged to him for the information; though I thought him mistaken as to the sameness of the experiment, the operations being different as well as the effects. In one case, the water is smooth till the oil is put on, and then becomes agitated. In the other it is agitated before the oil is applied, and then becomes smooth. The same gentleman told me, he had heard it was a practice with the fishermen of Lisbon when about to return into the river (if they saw before them too great a surf upon the bar, which they apprehended might fill their boats in passing) to empty a bottle or two of oil into the sea, which would suppress the breakers, and allow them to pass safely. A confirmation of this I have not since had an opportunity of obtaining; but discoursing of it with another person, who had often been in the Mediterranean, I was informed, that the divers there, who, when under water in their business, need light, which the curling of the surface interrupts by the refractions of so many little waves, let a small quantity of oil now and then out of their mouths, which rising to the surface smooths it, and permits the light to come down to them. All these informations I at times revolved in my mind, and wondered to find no mention of them in our books of experimental philosophy.

At length being at Clapham, where there is, on the common, a large pond, which I observed one day to be very rough with the wind, I fetched out a cruet of oil, and dropped a little of it on the water. I saw it spread itself with surprising swiftness upon the surface; but the effect of smoothing the waves was not produced; for I had applied it first on the leeward side of the pond, where the waves were largest, and the wind drove my oil back upon the shore. I then went to the windward side where they began to form; and there the oil, though not more than a tea spoonful, produced an instant calm over a space several yards square, which spread amazingly, and extended itself gradually till it reached the lee side, making all that quarter of the pond, perhaps half an acre, as smooth as a looking-glass.

After this I contrived to take with me, whenever I went into the country, a little oil in the upper hollow joint of my bamboo cane, with which I might repeat the experiment as opportunity should offer, and I found it constantly to succeed.

In these experiments, one circumstance struck me with particular surprise. This was the sudden, wide, and forcible spreading of a drop of oil on the face of the water, which I do not know that anybody has hitherto considered. If a drop of oil is put on a highly polished marble table, or on a looking-glass that lies horizontally, the drop remains in its place, spreading very little. But, when put on water, it spreads instantly, many feet round, becoming so thin as to produce the prismatic colors, for a considerable space, and beyond them so much thinner as to be invisible, except in its effect of smoothing the waves at a much greater distance. It seems as if a mutual repulsion between its particles took place as soon as it touched the water, and a repulsion so strong as to act on other bodies swimming on the surface, as straw, leaves, chips, &c. forcing them to recede every way from the drop, as from a centre, leaving a large, clear space. The quantity of this force, and the distance to which it will operate, I have not yet ascertained; but I think it a curious inquiry, and I wish to understand whence it arises.

In our journey to the North, when we had the pleasure of seeing you at Ormathwaite, we visited the celebrated Mr. Smeaton, near Leeds. Being about to show him the smoothing experiment on a little pond near his house, an ingenious pupil of his, Mr. Jessop, then present, told us of an odd appearance on that pond, which had lately occurred to him. He was about to clean a little cup in which he kept oil, and he threw upon the water some flies that had been drowned in the oil. These flies presently began to move, and turned round on the water very rapidly, as if they were vigorously alive, though on examination he found they were not so. I immediately concluded that the motion was occasioned by the power of the repulsion above mentioned, and that the oil issuing gradually from the spungy body of the fly continued the motion. He found some more flies drowned in oil, with which the experiment was repeated before us. To show that it was not any effect of life recovered by the flies, I imitated it by little bits of oiled chips and paper, cut in the form of a comma, of the size of a common fly; when the stream of repelling particles issuing from the point made the comma turn round the contrary way. This is not a chamber experiment; for it cannot be well repeated in a bowl or dish of water on a table. A considerable surface of water is necessary to give room for the expansion of a small quantity of oil. In a dish of water, if the smallest drop of oil be let fall in the middle, the whole surface is presently covered with a thin greasy film proceeding from the drop; but as soon as that film has reached the sides of the dish, no more will issue from the drop, but it remains in the form of oil, the sides of the dish putting a stop to its dissipation by prohibiting the farther expansion of the film.

Our friend Sir John Pringle, being soon after in Scotland, learned there, that those employed in the herring fishery could at a distance see where the shoals of herrings were, by the smoothness of the water over them, which might possibly be occasioned, he thought, by some oiliness proceeding from their bodies.

A gentleman from Rhode Island told me, it had been remarked, that the harbour of Newport was ever smooth while any whaling vessels were in it; which probably arose from hence, that the blubber which they sometimes bring loose in the hold, or the leakage of their barrels, might afford some oil, to mix with that water, which from time to time they pump out, to keep their vessel free, and that some oil might spread over the surface of the water in the harbour, and prevent the forming of any waves.

This prevention I would thus endeavour to explain.

There seems to be no natural repulsion between water and air, such as to keep them from coming into contact with each other. Hence we find a quantity of air in water; and if we extract it by means of the air-pump, the same water, again exposed to the air, will soon imbibe an equal quantity.

Therefore air in motion, which is wind, in passing over the smooth surface of water, may rub, as it were, upon that surface, and raise it into wrinkles, which, if the wind continues, are the elements of future waves.

The smallest wave once raised does not immediately subside, and leave the neighbouring water quiet; but in subsiding raises nearly as much of the water next to it, the friction of the parts making little difference. Thus a stone dropped in a pool raises first a single wave round itself; and leaves it, by sinking to the bottom; but that first wave subsiding raises a second, a second a third, and so on in circles to a great extent.

A small power continually operating will produce a great action. A finger applied to a weighty suspended bell can at first move it but little; if repeatedly applied, though with no greater strength, the motion increases till the bell swings to its utmost height, and with a force that cannot be resisted by the whole strength of the arm and body. Thus the small first-raised waves, being continually acted upon by the wind, are, though the wind does not increase in strength, continually increased in magnitude, rising higher and extending their basis, so as to include a vast mass of water in each wave, which in its motion acts with great violence.

But if there be a mutual repulsion between the particles of oil, and no attraction between oil and water, oil dropped on water will not be held together by adhesion to the spot whereon it falls; it will not be imbibed by the water; it will be at liberty to expand itself; and it will spread on a surface, that besides being smooth to the most perfect degree of polish, prevents, perhaps by repelling the oil, all immediate contact, keeping it at a minute distance from itself; and the expansion will continue till the mutual repulsion between the particles of the oil is weakened and reduced to nothing by their distance.

Now I imagine that the wind, blowing over water thus covered with a film of oil, cannot easily *catch* upon it, so as to raise the first wrinkles, but slides over it, and leaves it smooth as it finds it. It moves a little the oil indeed, which being between it and the water, serves it to slide with, and prevents friction, as oil does between those parts of a machine, that would otherwise rub hard together. Hence the oil dropped on the windward side of a pond proceeds gradually to leeward, as may be seen by the smoothness it carries with it, quite to the opposite side. For the wind being thus prevented from raising the first wrinkles, that I call the elements of waves, cannot produce waves, which are to be made by continually acting upon, and enlarging those elements, and thus the whole pond is calmed.

Totally therefore we might suppress the waves in any required place, if we could come at the windward place where they take their rise. This in the ocean can seldom if ever be done. But perhaps something may be done on particular occasions, to moderate the violence of the waves when we are in the midst of them, and prevent their breaking where that would be inconvenient.

For, when the wind blows fresh, there are continually rising on the back of every great wave a number of small ones, which roughen its surface, and give the wind hold, as it were, to push it with greater force. This hold is diminished, by preventing the generation of those small ones. And possibly too, when a wave's surface is oiled, the wind, in passing over it, may rather in some degree press it down, and contribute to prevent its rising again, instead of promoting it.

This, as mere conjecture, would have little weight, if the apparent effects of pouring oil into the midst of waves were not considerable, and as yet not otherwise accounted for.

When the wind blows so fresh, as that the waves are not sufficiently quick in obeying its impulse, their tops being thinner and lighter are pushed forward, broken, and turned over in a white foam. Common waves lift a vessel without entering it; but these when large sometimes break above and pour over it, doing great damage.

That this effect might in any degree be prevented, or the height and violence of waves in the sea moderated, we had no certain account; Pliny's authority for the practice of seamen in his time being slighted. But discoursing lately on this subject with his Excellency Count Bentinck, of Holland, his son the Honourable Captain Bentinck, and the learned Professor Allemand, (to all whom I showed the experiment of smoothing in a windy day the large piece of water at the head of the Green Park,) a letter was mentioned, which had been received by the Count from Batavia, relative to the saving of a Dutch ship in a storm by pouring oil into the sea. I much desired to see that letter, and a copy of it was promised me, which I afterward received.

Extract of a Letter from Mr. Tengnagel to Count Bentinck, dated at Batavia, 5 January, 1770

"Near the islands Paul and Amsterdam, we met with a storm, which had nothing particular in it worthy of being communicated to you, except that the captain found himself obliged for greater safety in wearing the ship, to pour oil into the sea, to prevent the waves breaking over her, which had an excellent effect, and succeeded in preserving us. As he poured out but a little at a time, the East India Company owes perhaps its ship to only six demi-ames of oil-olive. I was present upon deck when this was done; and I should not have mentioned this circumstance to you, but that we have found people here so prejudiced against the experiment, as to make it necessary for the officers on board and myself to give a certificate of the truth on this head, of which we made no difficulty."

On this occasion, I mentioned to Captain Bentinck a thought which had occurred to me in reading the voyages of our late circum-navigators, particularly where accounts are given of pleasant and fertile islands which they much desired to land upon, when sickness made it more necessary, but could not effect a landing through a violent surf breaking on the shore, which rendered it impracticable. My idea was, that possibly by sailing to and fro at some distance from such lee-shore, continually pouring oil into the sea, the waves might be so much depressed, and lessened before they reached the shore, as to abate the height and violence of the surf, and permit a landing; which, in such circumstances, was a point of sufficient importance to justify the expense of the oil that might be requisite for the purpose.

That gentleman, who is ever ready to promote what may be of public utility, though his own ingenious inventions have not always met with the countenance they merited, was so obliging as to invite me to Portsmouth, where an opportunity would probably offer, in the course of a few days, of making the experiment on some of the shores about Spithead, in which he kindly proposed to accompany me, and to give assistance with such boats as might be necessary. Accordingly, about the middle of October last, I went with some friends to Portsmouth; and a day of wind happening, which made a leeshore between Haslar hospital and the point near Jillkecker, we went from the Centaur with the longboat and barge towards that shore. Our disposition was this; the longboat was anchored about a quarter of a mile from the shore; part of the company were landed behind the point (a place more sheltered from the sea) who came round and placed themselves opposite to the longboat, where they might observe the surf and note if any change occurred in it upon using the oil. Another party, in the barge, plied to windward of the longboat, as far from her as she was from the shore, making trips of about half a mile each, pouring oil continually out of a large stone bottle, through a hole in the cork, somewhat bigger than a goose-quill. The experiment had not, in the main point, the success we wished, for no material difference was observed in the height or force of the surf upon the shore; but those who were in the longboat could observe a tract of smoothed water, the whole of the distance in which the barge poured the oil, and gradually spreading in breadth towards the longboat. I call it smoothed, not that it was laid level; but because, though the swell continued, its surface was not roughened by the wrinkles, or smaller waves, before mentioned; and none or very few white caps (or waves whose tops turn over in foam) appeared in that whole space, though to windward and leeward of it there were plenty; and a wherry, that came round the point under sail, in her way to Portsmouth, seemed to turn into that tract of choice, and to use it from end to end, as a piece of turnpike road.

It may be of use to relate the circumstances of an experiment that does not succeed, since they may give hints of amendment in future trials;

it is therefore I have been thus particular. I shall only add what I apprehend may have been the reason of our disappointment.

I conceive, that the operation of oil on water is, first, to prevent the raising of new waves by the wind; and, secondly, to prevent its pushing those before raised with such force, and consequently their continuance of the same repeated height, as they would have done, if their surface were not oiled. But oil will not prevent waves being raised by another power, by a stone, for instance, falling into a still pool; for they then rise by the mechanical impulse of the stone, which the greasiness on the surrounding water cannot lessen or prevent, as it can prevent the winds catching the surface and raising it into waves. Now waves once raised, whether by the wind or any other power, have the same mechanical operation, by which they continue to rise and fall, as a *pendulum* will continue to swing a long time after the force ceases to act by which the motion was first produced; that motion will, however, cease in time; but time is necessary. Therefore, though oil spread on an agitated sea may weaken the push of the wind on those waves whose surfaces are covered by it, and so, by receiving less fresh impulse, they may gradually subside; yet a considerable time, or a distance through which they will take time to move, may be necessary to make the effect sensible on any shore in a diminution of the surf; for we know, that, when wind ceases suddenly, the waves it has raised do not as suddenly subside, but settle gradually, and are not quite down till after the wind has ceased. So, though we should, by oiling them, take off the effect of wind on waves already raised, it is not to be expected that those waves should be instantly levelled. The motion they have received will, for some time, continue; and, if the shore is not far distant, they arrive there so soon, that their effect upon it will not be visibly diminished. Possibly, therefore, if we had begun our operations at a greater distance, the effect might have been more sensible. And perhaps we did not pour oil in sufficient quantity. Future experiments may determine this.

I was, however, greatly obliged to Captain Bentinck, for the cheerful and ready aids he gave me; and I ought not to omit mentioning Mr. Banks, Dr. Solander, General Carnoc, and Dr. Blagden, who all assisted at the experiment, during that blustering, unpleasant day, with a patience and activity that could only be inspired by a zeal for the improvement of knowledge, such especially as might possibly be of use to men in situations of distress.

(b) Model Basin

Franklin designed a miniature towing tank and performed an experiment in it to test the drag of a model drawn in the water of a canal as a function of its depth. There was a definite increase as the water became more shallow. Scaling, however, is always a problem in a gravitational field; it is aggravated by the presence of a free surface. Such empirical hydraulics had to be supplemented later with mathematical hydraulics about the middle of the nineteenth century.

To JOHN PRINGLE. May 10, 1768

You may remember, that when we were travelling together in *Holland*, you remarked, that the trackschuyt in one of the stages went slower than usual, and inquired of the boatman, what might be the reason; who answered, that it had been a dry season, and the water in the canal was low. On being again asked if it was so low as that the boat touched the muddy bottom; he said, no, not so low as that, but so low as to make it harder for the horse to draw the boat. We neither of us at first could conceive that if there was water enough for the boat to swim clear of the bottom, its being deeper would make any difference; but as the man affirmed it seriously as a thing well known among them; and as the punctuality required in their stages, was likely to make such difference, if any there were, more readily observed by them, than by other watermen who did not pass so regularly and constantly backwards and forwards in the same track; I began to apprehend there might be something in it, and attempted to account for it from this consideration, that the boat in proceeding along the canal, must in every boat's length of her course, move out of her way a body of water, equal in bulk to the room her bottom took up in the water; that the water so moved, must pass on each side of her and under her bottom to get behind her; that if the passage under her bottom was straitened by the shallows, more of that water must pass by her sides, and with a swifter motion, which would retard her, as moving the contrary way; or that the water becoming lower behind the boat than before, she was pressed back by the weight of its difference in height, and her motion retarded by having that weight constantly to overcome. But as it is often lost time to attempt accounting for uncertain facts, I determined to make an experiment of this, when I should have convenient time and opportunity.

After our return to *England*, as often as I happened to be on the *Thames*, I inquired of our watermen whether they were sensible of any difference in rowing over shallow or deep water. I found them all agreeing in the fact, that there was a very great difference, but they differed widely in expressing the quantity of the difference; some supposing it was equal to a mile in six, others to a mile in three, &c. As I did not recollect to have met with any mention of this matter in our philosophical books, and conceiving that if the difference should really be great, it might be an object of consideration in the many projects now on foot for digging new navigable canals in this island, I lately put my design of making the experiment in execution, in the following manner.

I provided a trough of plained boards fourteen feet long, six inches wide and six inches deep, in the clear, filled with water within half an inch of the edge, to represent a canal. I had a loose board of nearly the same length and breadth, that being put into the water might be sunk to any depth, and fixed by little wedges where I would chuse to have it stay, in order to make different depths of water, leaving the surface at the same height with regard to the sides of the trough. I had a little boat in form of a lighter or boat of burthen, six inches long, two inches and a quarter wide, and one inch and a quarter deep. When swimming, it drew one inch water. To give motion to the boat, I fixed one end of a long silk thread to its bow, just even with the water's edge, the other end passed over a well made brass pully, of about an inch diameter, turning freely on a small axis; and a shilling was the weight. Then placing the boat at one end of the trough, the weight would draw it through the water to the other.

Not having a watch that shows seconds, in order to measure the time taken up by the boat in passing from end to end, I counted as fast as I could count to ten repeatedly, keeping an account of the number of tens on my fingers. And as much as possible to correct any little inequalities in my counting, I repeated the experiment a number of times at each depth of water, that I might take the medium. And the following are the results.

Water 1½ inches deep.		2 inches.	4½ inches.
1st exp.	100	94	79
2	104	93	78
3	104	91	77
4	106	87	79
5	100	88	79
6	99	86	80
7	100	90	79
8	100	88	81
	813	717	632
	Medium 101	Medium 89	Medium 79

I made many other experiments, but the above are those in which I was most exact; and they serve sufficiently to show that the difference is considerable. Between the deepest and shallowest it appears to be somewhat more than one fifth. So that supposing large canals and boats and depths of water to bear the same proportions, and that four men or horses would draw a boat in deep water four leagues in four hours, it would require five to draw the same boat in the same time as far in shallow water; or four would require five hours.

Whether this difference is of consequence enough to justify a greater expence in deepening canals, is a matter of calculation, which our ingenious engineers in that way will readily determine.

CHAPTER 7

Amber and Glass

WHEN Franklin's interest in electric phenomena was aroused in 1747, four experiential facts were currently known.

In the first place, the attraction of rubbed amber (Greek, electron) for light materials had been known since antiquity, e.g. Thales of Miletus (*c.* 640–546 BC), one of the Seven Wise Men of Greece. The Greek philosopher and botanist Theophrastus (373–287 BC), who succeeded Aristotle as head of the Lyceum, had called attention to a similar electrification (made like amber) of jet and onyx. The Italian physician Girolamo Fracastoro (1483–1553) added diamond to the list. The Italian mathematician and physician Geronimo Cardano (1501–76) had noted the difference of this kind of attraction and that of magnetism. The English physician to Elizabeth I, William Gilbert (1540–1603) of Colchester, father of magnetism, listed a large number electrics (like amber) such as glass, precious stones, and sealing wax. It was generally believed that the phenomenon was owing to the release by friction of fluid similar to body humors. Attraction would then be the result of the contact with the effuvia atmosphere thus produced. The English physician and author Sir Thomas Browne (1605–82), who introduced the term electricity, noted in 1646 some additional substances. The Irish natural philosopher Robert Boyle (1627–91) observed that the phenomenon occurs even in a vacuum, and Newton himself noted that the effect takes place through plate glass. The French scientist Charles François de Cisternay du Fay (1638–1739) concluded that most nonmetallic materials are electric. In 1660 the German physicist Otto von Guericke (1602–86) made the first electric machine, i.e. a 6-inch sulphur ball mounted on a wooden axle; it could be rubbed by hand. The English physicist Francis Hauksbee (d. *c.* 1713), curator of instruments for the Royal Society of London, used a glass globe (rubbed with flannel) attached by a chain to an insulated metal such as a gunbarrel. After a period of neglect, interest was revived in 1744 when a "rubber" (made of leather and stuffed cushions) was added by the German Johann Heinrich Winkler (1703–1770).

The second primary fact known was repulsion. About 1629–30 the Italian Jesuit Nicolò Cabeo (1585–1650) noted that light objects are attracted and then repelled after contact with an electrified body— first published by von Guericke. du Fay observed further that rubbed amber, when pivoted, would experience attraction with some electrified materials, but repulsion with others. He concluded, in 1733, that there were actually two electric fluids—resinous (like amber) and vitreous (like glass). Abbé Jean-Antoine Nollet (1700–70), a pupil of du Fay, a teacher of natural philosophy at L'École de Mézières and preceptor to the Dauphin (Louis XVI), offered as an explanation that one fluid was affluent (moving toward a body) and the other effluent (moving away from it). Attraction and repulsion of light bodies resulted from their being caught in the one stream or the other, respectively.

Thirdly, the conduction of electricity had been discovered. von Guericke, for example, had found that attraction would be transmitted to some degree through a linen thread. The chief investigations, however, were made by Stephen Gray (d. 1736), a pensioner of Charterhouse; one experiment (1730), repeated at Philadelphia in 1744, involved drawing a spark from the nose of a suspended boy when his feet were rubbed with a piece of glass. Gray distinguished between a conductor and an insulator as being, respectively, a nonelectric and an electric. Electric effects, for example, were observed to be transferred by wires— but not by silk threads—over a distance as great as 765 ft. For the first time electricity exhibited true fluidity; it was not just static. Certain electric phenomena that had seemed capricious, even mysterious, were now explained as a matter of leakage.

The last basic fact was electric storage, discovered accidentally by Musschenbroek in 1746. In attempting to store electric charges in a phial containing a gunbarrel inserted in water, a friend—grasping the phial with one hand and the gunbarrel with the other—received a severe shock; evidently electric charge had been stored. It became a fashion to demonstrate the effect publicly. A spectacular occasion was the passing of an electric charge through Carthusian Monks in Paris, lined up hand-in-hand for some 900 ft. Watson discovered that the strength of the discharge could be increased by coating the outside of a jar with tin foil. (Nowadays the inside is also coated with tin foil.) Ewald Georg Kleist (d. 1748), Dean of the Cathedral of Kamin, Pomerania, who discovered the effect independently (possibly earlier), had put a nail in a phial containing alcohol. The Leyden jar soon became a powerful tool for investigating electric so-called phenomena.

(a) Conservation of Electric Charge

In his first letter reporting his electric investigations to Collinson, Franklin described a fundamental experiment and outlined his one-fluid theory in terms of his own nomenclature.

He considered three men, each placed upon a separate cake of wax (an insulator). The first man rubbed a glass tube and passed a spark to the second; each was then able to pass a spark to the third. If the first two touched each other after the electrification, they both became neutralized—exemplified later in the case of a charged Leyden jar.

Franklin assumed that there is a single electric fluid, which is particulate and subtle, elastic and self-repellent. Matter normally holds a certain amount of it, which becomes evident only upon rubbing—like squeezing a sponge saturated with water. The fluid is not produced by friction; it is merely separated from its usual location. A body with an excess is said to be positively charged (loaded); a body with a deficiency, negatively. An excess supposedly produced an atmosphere about the surface like the smoke from a body with dry resin on it.

Franklin's theory had the virtue of dealing with only two substances—matter and electricity—rather than with three—matter and two kinds of electricity. Moreover, it inherently assumed the conservation of electric charge, as when a pile of earth has the same volume as the hole from which it has been dug—one of the fundamental principles of modern physics. There was, however, one troublesome question, namely how could one account for the repulsion of two fluidless, i.e. negatively charged, bodies—matter *per se* usually attracts matter (gravitation). The German natural philosopher Franz Maria Ulrich Theodor Aepinus (1724–1802), who settled in St. Petersburg, modified Franklin's theory in 1759 by postulating additionally the self-repulsion of negatively charged matter, thus nullifying the apparent gain in simplicity by virtually adding a second nonfluid electric. Robert Symmer (d. 1763) suggested in 1759 that electrification merely signified the separation of a normally neutral mixture of the two fluids.

Franklin had initially regarded the vitreous fluid as the positive electric fluid. Why? Because the vitreous charge seemed to spread over an opposite conductor. A candle-flame, moreover, appeared to be blown away by a vitreous charged body, but toward a resinous charged one. (The sign of the charge on an electrified body depends not only upon the nature of the body itself but also upon the nature of the rubbing body. Substances can be arranged in an electropositive-electronegative series.) Aepinus eliminated effluvia as such, inasmuch as the electric fluid was apparently not carried off with air that was blown away. The eighteenth century ended with a dilemma posed by electric conduction in solids: both the one-fluid theory and the two-fluid theory were adequate to explain such phenomena. Incidentally, Lavoisier included electricity as a chemical element, together with heat and light, in his epoch-making *Elementary Treatise of Chemistry* in 1789, which established a quantitative basis for chemistry.

Another dilemma arose in 1833 as a result of the English physicist and chemist Michael Faraday's investigations of the conduction of electricity in liquids: Is an electric fluid continuous or is it made up of discrete units? The answer to both dilemmas emerged out of the neglected field of the conduction of electricity in gases. J. J. Thomson

(1897) showed that there is a small discrete particle, the electron, which is negatively charged and is somewhat free to move in metals, whereas the more massive, positively charged ions remain localized. The electric current of today, which by definition flows from a positive terminal, actually consists of a drift of electrons in the opposite direction. As Thomson remarked in 1936, "A collection of electrons would resemble in many respects Franklin's electric fluid." It is still particularly useful nowadays for qualitative thinking. If one were asked today what would happen if a piece of glass that had been rubbed with silk were brought near another piece of glass rubbed with silk, one would never seek the answer by solving the French mathematician Siméon Denis Poisson's (1781–1840) partial differential equation of electrostatics.

Probably Franklin's greatest contribution was his design of experiments for testing scientific hypotheses; he himself showed a mastery of laboratory techniques. He admitted to the Massachusetts physician John Perkins (1698–1781) in a letter (August 13, 1752): "I own I have too strong a penchant to the building of hypotheses; they indulge my natural indolence." Many of his experimental practices are commonplace in physics today, for example the use of a semicircular wire with an insulated handle for discharging—not to mention electrical terminology itself.

Franklin's views were not immediately accepted by all those interested in science. The most notable opponent was the French professor of physics Nollet who had amended his mentor du Fay's two fluids to be continuously in motion, namely, affluent and effluent, respectively. In 1753 he formulated his arguments in a book consisting of nine essays, including six letters directed to Franklin, who found difficulty verifying some of the cited experimental data. Before Franklin himself could respond, satisfactory replies had been made in 1753 by the loyalist physician David Colden (1733–84), son of Franklin's friend Cadwallader, and by the Italian professor of experimental physics, Beccaria.

To Peter Collinson. *July 11, 1747*

In my last I informed you that, in pursuing our electrical enquiries, we had observed some particular phænomena, which we looked upon to be new, and of which I promised to give you some account, though I apprehended they might possibly not be new to you, as so many hands are daily employed in electrical experiments on your side the water, some or other of which would probably hit on the same observations.

The first is the wonderful effect of pointed bodies, both in *drawing off* and *throwing off* the electrical fire. For example.

Place an iron shot of three or four inches diameter on the mouth of a clean dry glass bottle. By a fine silken thread from the cieling, right over the mouth of the bottle, suspend a small cork ball, about the bigness of a marble; the thread of such a length, as that the cork ball may rest against the side of the shot. Electrify the shot, and the ball will be repelled to the distance of four or five inches, more or less, according to the quantity of Electricity. When in this state, if you present to the shot the point of a long slender sharp bodkin, at six or eight inches distance, the repellency is instantly destroy'd, and the cork flies to the shot. A blunt body must be brought within an inch, and draw a spark, to produce the same effect. To prove that the electrical fire is *drawn off* by the point, if you take the blade of the bodkin out of the wooden handle, and fix it in a stick of sealing-wax, and then present it at the distance aforesaid, or if you bring it very near, no such effect follows; but sliding one finger along the wax till you touch the blade, and the ball flies to the shot immediately. If you present the point in the dark, you will see, sometimes at a foot distance, and more, a light gather upon it, like that of a fire-fly, or glow-worm; the less sharp the point, the nearer you must bring it to observe the light; and, at whatever distance you see the light, you may draw off the electrical fire, and destroy the repellency. If a cork ball so suspended be repelled by the tube, and a point be presented quick to it, tho' at a considerable distance, 'tis surprizing to see how suddenly it flies back to the tube. Points of wood will do near as well as those of iron, provided the wood is not dry; for perfectly dry wood will no more conduct Electricity than sealing-wax.

To shew that points will *throw off*[1] as well as *draw off* the electrical fire; lay a long sharp needle upon the shot, and you cannot electrise the shot so as to make it repel the rock ball.[2] Or fix a needle to the end of a suspended gun-barrel, or iron rod, so as to point beyond it like a little bayonet; and while it remains there, the gun-barrel, or rod, cannot by applying the tube to the other end be electrised so as to give a spark, the fire continually running out silently at the point. In the dark you may see it make the same appearance as it does in the case before mentioned.

The repellency between the cork ball and the shot is likewise destroyed. 1, by sifting fine sand on it; this does it gradually. 2, by breathing on it. 3, by making a smoke about it from burning wood.[3] 4, by candle-light, even though the candle is at a foot distance: these do it suddenly. The light of a bright coal from a wood fire; and the light of red-hot iron do it likewise; but not at so great a distance. Smoke from dry rosin dropt on hot iron, does not destroy the repellency; but is attracted by both shot and cork ball, forming proportionable atmospheres round them, making them look beautifully, somewhat like some of the figures in *Burnet's* or *Whiston's Theory of the Earth.*

N.B. This experiment should be made in a closet, where the air is very still, or it will be apt to fail.

---

[1] This power of points to *throw off* the electrical fire, was first communicated to me by my ingenious friend, Mr. *Thomas Hopkinson,* since deceased, whose virtue and integrity, in every station of life, public and private, will ever make his Memory dear to those who knew him, and knew how to value him.

[2] This was Mr. *Hopkinson's* experiment, made with an expectation of drawing a more sharp and powerful spark from the point, as from a kind of focus, and he was surprized to find little or none.

[3] We suppose every particle of sand, moisture, or smoke, being first attracted and then repelled, carries off with it a portion of the electrical fire; but that the same still subsists in those particles, till they communicate it to something else, and that it is never really destroyed. So, when water is thrown on common fire, we do not imagine the element is thereby destroyed or annihilated, but only dispersed, each particle of water carrying off in vapour its portion of the fire, which it had attracted and attached to itself.

The light of the sun thrown strongly on both cork and shot by a looking-glass for a long time together, does not impair the repellency in the least. This difference between fire-light and sun-light is another thing that seems new and extraordinary to us.[1]

We had for some time been of opinion, that the electrical fire was not created by friction, but collected, being really an element diffus'd among, and attracted by other matter, particularly by water and metals. We had even discovered and demonstrated its afflux to the electrical sphere, as well as its efflux, by means of little light windmill-wheels made of stiff paper vanes, fixed obliquely and turning freely on fine wire axes; also by little wheels of the same matter, but formed like water-wheels. Of the disposition and application of which wheels, and the various phænomena resulting, I could, if I had time, fill you a sheet.[2] The impossibility of electrising one's self (though standing on wax) by rubbing the tube, and drawing the fire from it; and the manner of doing it, by passing the tube near a person or thing standing on the floor, &c., had also occurred to us some months before Mr. *Watson's* ingenious *Sequel* came to hand, and these were some of the new things I intended to have communicated to you. But now I need only mention some particulars not hinted in that piece, with our reasonings thereupon; though perhaps the latter might well enough be spared.

1. A person standing on wax, and rubbing the tube, and another person on wax drawing the fire, they will both of them, (provided they do not stand so as to touch one another) appear to be electrised, to a person standing on the floor; that is, he will perceive a spark on approaching each of them with his knuckle.

---

[1] This different Effect probably did not arise from any difference in the light, but rather from the particles separated from the candle, being first attracted and then repelled, carrying off the electric matter with them; and from the rarefying the air, between the glowing coal or red-hot iron, and the electrised shot, through which rarefied air the electric fluid could more readily pass.

[2] These experiments with the wheels were made and communicated to me by my worthy and ingenious friend, Mr. *Philip Syng;* but we afterwards discovered, that the motion of those wheels was not owing to any afflux or efflux of the electric fluid, but to various circumstances of attraction and repulsion.

2. But, if the persons on wax touch one another during the exciting of the tube, neither of them will appear to be electrised.

3. If they touch one another after exciting the tube, and drawing the fire as aforesaid, there will be a stronger spark between them, than was between either of them and the person on the floor.

4. After such strong spark, neither of them discover any electricity.

These appearances we attempt to account for thus: We suppose, as aforesaid, that electrical fire is a common element, of which every one of the three persons above mentioned has his equal share, before any operation is begun with the tube. *A*, who stands on wax and rubs the tube, collects the electrical fire from himself into the glass; and his communication with the common stock being cut off by the wax, his body is not again immediately supply'd. *B*, (who stands on wax likewise) passing his knuckle along near the tube, receives the fire which was collected by the glass from *A*; and his communication with the common stock being likewise cut off, he retains the additional quantity received. To *C*, standing on the floor, both appear to be electrised: for he having only the middle quantity of electrical fire, receives a spark upon approaching *B*, who has an over quantity; but gives one to *A*, who has an under quantity. If *A* and *B* approach to touch each other, the spark is stronger, because the difference between them is greater: After such touch there is no spark between either of them and *C*, because the electrical fire in all is reduced to the original equality. If they touch while electrising, the equality is never destroy'd, the fire only circulating. Hence have arisen some new terms among us: we say, *B*, (and bodies like circumstanced) is electrised *positively; A, negatively.* Or rather, *B* is electrised *plus*; *A, minus.* And we daily in our experiments electrise bodies *plus or minus*, as we think proper. To electrise *plus* or *minus*, no more needs to be known than this, that the parts of the tube or sphere that are rubbed, do, in the instant of the friction, attract the electrical fire, and therefore take it from the thing rubbing: the same parts immediately, as the friction upon them ceases, are disposed to give the fire they have received, to any body that has less. Thus you may circulate it, as Mr. *Watson* has shewn; you may also accumulate or subtract it upon, or from any body, as you connect that body with the rubber or with the receiver, the communication with the common stock being cut off. We think that ingenious gentleman was deceived when he imagined (in his *Sequel*) that the electrical fire came down the wire from the cieling to the gun-barrel, thence to the sphere, and so electrised the machine and the man turning the wheel, &c. We suppose it was *driven off*, and not brought on through that wire; and that the machine and man, &c., were electrised *minus*, i.e. had less electrical fire in them than things in common.

As the vessel is just upon sailing, I cannot give you so large an account of *American* electricity as I intended: I shall only mention a few particulars more. We find granulated lead better to fill the phial with, than water, being easily warmed, and keeping warm and dry in damp air. We fire spirits with the wire of the phial. We light candles, just blown out, by drawing a spark among the smoke, between the wire and snuffers. We represent lightning, by passing the wire in the dark, over a China plate, that has gilt flowers, or applying it to gilt frames of looking-glasses, &c. We electrise a person twenty or more times running, with a touch of the finger on the wire, thus: He stands on wax. Give him the electrised bottle in his hand. Touch the wire with your finger, and then touch his hand or face; there are sparks every time.[1] We increase the force of the electrical kiss vastly, thus: Let *A* and *B* stand on wax; or *A* on wax, and *B* on the floor; give one of them the electrised phial in hand; let the other take hold of the wire; there will be a small spark; but when their lips approach, they will be struck and shock'd. The same if another gentleman and lady, *C* and *D*, standing also on wax, and joining hands with *A* and *B*, salute or shake hands. We suspend by fine silk thread a counterfeit spider, made of a small piece of burnt cork, with legs of linnen thread, and a grain or two of lead stuck in him, to give him more weight. Upon the table, over which he hangs, we stick a wire upright,

---

[1] By taking a spark from the wire, the electricity within the bottle is diminished; the outside of the bottle then draws some from the person holding it, and leaves him in the negative state. Then when his hand or face is touch'd, an equal quantity is restored to him from the person touching.

as high as the phial and wire, two or three inches from the spider: then we animate him, by setting the electrified phial at the same distance on the other side of him; he will immediately fly to the wire of the phial, bend his legs in touching it; then spring off, and fly to the wire on the table; thence again to the wire of the phial, playing with his legs against both, in a very entertaining manner, appearing perfectly alive to persons unacquainted. He will continue this motion an hour or more in dry weather. We electrify, upon wax in the dark, a book that has a double line of gold round upon the covers, and then apply a knuckle to the gilding; the fire appears everywhere upon the gold like a flash of lightning: not upon the leather, nor, if you touch the leather instead of the gold. We rub our tubes with buckskin, and observe always to keep the same side to the tube, and never to sully the tube by handling; thus they work readily and easily, without the least fatigue, especially if kept in tight pasteboard cases, lined with flannel, and sitting close to the tube.[1] This I mention, because the *European* papers on Electricity, frequently speak of rubbing the tube, as a fatiguing exercise. Our spheres are fixed on iron axes, which pass through them. At one end of the axis there is a small handle, with which you turn the sphere like a common grindstone. This we find very commodious, as the machine takes up but little room, is portable, and may be enclosed in a tight box, when not in use. 'Tis true, the sphere does not turn so swift as when the great wheel is used: but swiftness we think of little importance, since a few turns will charge the phial, &c., sufficiently.[2]

(b) Leyden Jar

Franklin discovered how to electrify a conductor permanently first by inducing (no contact) charge on it and then grounding it. In this case the conductor will have an electric charge opposite to that of the inducing body. He was thus able to explain the action of a

---

[1] Our tubes are made here of green glass, 27 or 30 inches long, as big as can be grasped.

[2] This simple, easily-made machine was a contrivance of Mr. *Syng's*.

charged Leyden jar; he noted that the inside and outside were charged the same amount but oppositely. In the case of a pane of glass between two metal plates (the so-called parallel-plate condenser) only small sparks would be produced upon discharge if the glass were removed, as contrasted with the large spark with the glass in place—the role of the dielectric was later investigated by Faraday. In this connection, Franklin noted in 1753 that by varying the amount of brass chain hanging inside a silver can he could change the amount of electric charge that could be stored there—what we now call the effect of capacitance.

To PETER COLLINSON. *September 1, 1747*

The necessary trouble of copying long letters, which perhaps, when they come to your hands, may contain nothing new, or worth your reading, (so quick is the progress made with you in Electricity,) half discourages me from writing any more on that subject. Yet I cannot forbear adding a few observations on M. *Muschenbroek's* wonderful bottle.

1. The non-electric contain'd in the bottle differs when electrised from a non-electric electrised out of the bottle, in this: that the electrical fire of the latter is accumulated *on its surface*, and forms an electrical atmosphere round it of considerable extent; but the electrical fire is crowded *into the substance* of the former, the glass confining it.[1]

2. At the same time that the wire and the top of the bottle, &c. is electrised *positively* or *plus*, the bottom of the bottle is electrised *negatively* or *minus*, in exact proportion; i.e., whatever quantity of electrical fire is thrown in at the top, an equal quantity goes out of the bottom.[2] To understand this, suppose the common quantity of

[1] See this opinion rectified § 16 and 17 [of letter dated April 27, 1749]. The fire in the bottle was found by subsequent experiments not to be contained in the non-electric, but *in the glass*. 1748.

[2] What is said here, and after, of the *top* and *bottom* of the bottle, is true of the *inside* and *outside* surfaces, and should have been so expressed.

electricity in each part of the bottle, before the operation begins, is equal to 20; and at every stroke of the tube, suppose a quantity equal to 1 is thrown in; then, after the first stroke, the quantity contained in the wire and upper part of the bottle will be 21, in the bottom 19; after the second, the upper part will have 22, the lower 18, and so on, till, after 20 strokes, the upper part will have a quantity of electrical fire equal to 40, the lower part none; and then the operation ends: for no more can be thrown into the upper part, when no more can be driven out of the lower part. If you attempt to throw more in, it is spued back through the wire, or flies out in loud cracks through the sides of the bottle.

3. The equilibrium cannot be restored in the bottle by *inward* communication or contact of the parts; but it must be done by a communication form'd *without* the bottle, between the top and bottom, by some non-electric, touching or approaching both at the same time; in which case it is restored with a violence and quickness inexpressible; or touching each alternately, in which case the equilibrium is restored by degrees.

4. As no more electrical fire can be thrown into the top of the bottle, when all is driven out of the bottom, so, in a bottle not yet electrised, none can be thrown into the top, when none *can* get out at the bottom; which happens either when the bottom is too thick, or when the bottle is placed on an electric *per se*. Again, when the bottle is electrised, but little of the electrical fire can be *drawn out* from the top, by touching the wire, unless an equal quantity can at the same time *get in* at the bottom.[1] Thus, place an electrised bottle on clean glass or dry wax, and you will not, by touching the wire, get out the fire from the top. Place it on a non-electric, and touch the wire, you will get it out in a short time; but soonest when you form a direct communication as above.

So wonderfully are these two states of electricity, the *plus* and *minus*, combined and balanced in this miraculous bottle! situated and related to each other in a manner that I can by no means comprehend!

---

[1] See the preceding note, relating to *top* and *bottom*.

If it were possible that a bottle should in one part contain a quantity of air strongly comprest, and in another part a perfect vacuum, we know the equilibrium would be instantly restored *within*. But here we have a bottle containing at the same time a *plenum* of electrical fire, and a *vacuum* of the same fire; and yet the equilibrium cannot be restored between them but by a communication *without!* though the *plenum* presses violently to expand, and the hungry vacuum seems to attract as violently in order to be filled.

5. The shock to the nerves (or convulsion rather) is occasioned by the sudden passing of the fire through the body in its way from the top to the bottom of the bottle. The fire takes the shortest course, as Mr. Watson justly observes. But it does not appear from experiment, that, in order for a person to be shocked, a communication with the floor is necessary; for he that holds the bottle with one hand, and touches the wire with the other, will be shock'd as much, though his shoes be dry, or even standing on wax, as otherwise. And, on the touch of the wire (or of the gunbarrel, which is the same thing), the fire does not proceed from the touching finger to the wire, as is supposed, but from the wire to the finger, and passes through the body to the other hand, and so into the bottom of the bottle.

Experiments confirming the above

EXPERIMENT I

Place an electrised phial on wax; a small cork ball, suspended by a dry silk-thread, held in your hand, and brought near to the wire, will first be attracted, and then repelled: when in this state of repellency, sink your hand, that the ball may be brought towards the bottom of the bottle; it will be there instantly and strongly attracted, 'till it has parted with its fire.

If the bottle had a *positive* electrical atmosphere, as well as the wire, an electrified cork would be repelled from one as well as from the other.

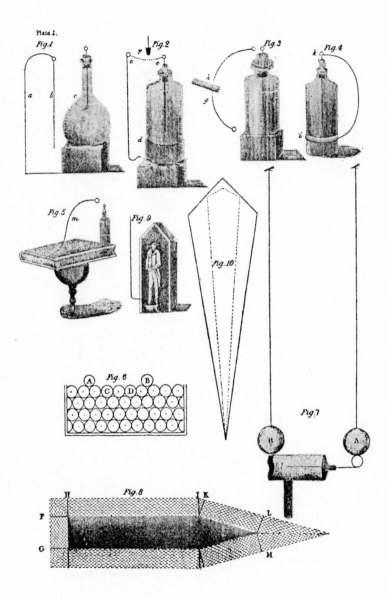

Plate I.

Fig.1 Fig.2 Fig.3 Fig.4

Fig.5 Fig.9

Fig.10

Fig.6

Fig.7

Fig.8

EXPERIMENT II

PL. I. FIG. 1. From a bent wire (*a*) sticking in the table, let a small linen thread (*b*) hang down within half an inch of the electrised phial (*c*). Touch the wire of the phial repeatedly with your finger, and at every touch you will see the thread instantly attracted by the bottle. (This is best done by a vinegar-cruet, or some such belly'd bottle.) As soon as you draw any fire out from the upper part by touching the wire, the lower part of the bottle draws an equal quantity in by the thread.

EXPERIMENT III

FIG. 2. Fix a wire in the lead, with which the bottom of the bottle is armed (*d*), so as that bending upwards, its ring-end may be level with the top or ring-end of the wire in the cork (*e*), and at three or four inches distance. Then electricise the bottle, and place it on wax. If a cork, suspended by a silk thread (*f*), hang between these two wires, it will play incessantly from one to the other, till the bottle is no long- er electrised; that is, it fetches and carries fire from the top to the bottom of the bottle, till the equilibrium is restored.

EXPERIMENT IV

FIG. 3. Place an electrised phial on wax; take a wire (*g*) in form of a C, the ends at such a distance when bent, as that the upper may touch the wire of the bottle, when the lower touches the bottom: stick the outer part on a stick of sealing-wax (*h*), which will serve as a handle; then apply the lower end to the bottom of the bottle, and gradually bring the upper end near the wire in the cork. The consequence is, spark follows spark till the equilibrium is restored. Touch the top first, and, on approaching the bottom with the other end, you have a constant stream of fire from the wire entering the bottle. Touch the top and bottom together, and the equilibrium will instantly be resto- red, the crooked wire forming the communication.

EXPERIMENT V

FIG. 4. Let a ring of thin lead, or paper, surround a bottle (*i*), even at some distance from or above the bottom. From that ring let a wire proceed up, till it touch the wire of the cork (*k*). A bottle so fixt cannot by any means be electrised: the equilibrium is never destroyed: for while the communication between the upper and lower parts of the bottle is continued by the outside wire, the fire only circulates; what is driven out at bottom, is constantly supply'd from the top.[1] Hence a bottle cannot be electrised, that is foul or moist on the outside, if such moisture continue up to the cork or wire.

EXPERIMENT VI

Place a man on a cake of wax, and present him the wire of the electrified phial to touch, you standing on the floor, and holding it in your hand. As often as he touches it, he will be electrified *plus;* and any one standing on the floor may draw a spark from him. The fire in this experiment passes out of the wire into him; and at the same time out of your hand into the bottom of the bottle.

EXPERIMENT VII

Give him the electrical phial to hold; and do you touch the wire; as often as you touch it, he will be electrified *minus*, and may draw a spark from any one standing on the floor. The fire now passes from the wire to you, and from him into the bottom of the bottle.

EXPERIMENT VIII

Lay two books on two glasses, back towards back, two or three inches distant. Set the electrified phial on one, and then touch the wire; that book will be electrified *minus;* the electrical fire being drawn out of it by the bottom of the bottle. Take off the bottle, and, holding it in your hand, touch the other with the wire; that book will be electri-

---

[1] *i.e.* from the inside to the outside.

fied *plus;* the fire passing into it from the wire, and the bottle at the same time supplied from your hand. A suspended small cork ball will play between these books 'till the equilibrium is restored.

EXPERIMENT IX

When a body is electrised *plus*, it will repel a positively electrified feather or small cork ball. When *minus* (or when in the common state), it will attract them, but stronger when *minus* than when in the common state, the difference being greater.

EXPERIMENT X

Though, as in *Experiment* VI, a man standing on wax may be electrised a number of times by repeatedly touching the wire of an electrised bottle (held in the hand of one standing on the floor), he receiving the fire from the wire each time: yet holding it in his own hand, and touching the wire, though he draws a strong spark, and is violently shocked, no Electricity remains in him; the fire only passing through him, from the upper to the lower part of the bottle. Observe, before the shock, to let some one on the floor touch him to restore the equilibrium in his body; for in taking hold of the bottom of the bottle, he sometimes becomes a little electrised *minus*, which will continue after the shock, as would also any *plus* Electricity, which he might have given him before the shock. For, restoring the equilibrium in the bottle does not at all effect the Electricity in the man through whom the fire passes; that Electricity is neither increased nor diminished.

EXPERIMENT XI

The passing of the electrical fire from the upper to the lower part[1] of the bottle, to restore the equilibrium, is rendered strongly visible by the following pretty experiment. Take a book whose covering is

---

[1] That is, from the *inside* to the *outside*.

filletted with gold; bend a wire of eight or ten inches long, in the form of (*m*), Fig. 5; slip it on the end of the cover of the book, over the gold line, so as that the shoulder of it may press upon one end of the gold line, the ring up, but leaning towards the other end of the book. Lay the book on a glass or wax, and on the other end of the gold lines set the bottle electrised; then bend the springing wire, by pressing it with a stick of wax, till its ring approaches the ring of the bottle wire; instantly there is a strong spark and stroke, and the whole line of gold, which completes the communication between the top and bottom of the bottle, will appear a vivid flame, like the sharpest lightning. The closer the contact between the shoulder of the wire and the gold at one end of the line, and between the bottom of the bottle and the gold at the other end, the better the experiment succeeds. The room should be darkened. If you would have the whole filletting round the cover appear in fire at once, let the bottle and wire touch the gold in the diagonally opposite corners.

To PETER COLLINSON. *April 29, 1749*

§ 1. There will be the same explosion and shock if the electrified phial is held in one hand by the hook, and the coating touch'd with the other, as when held by the coating, and touch'd at the hook.

2. To take the charg'd phial safely by the hook, and not at the same time diminish its force, it must first be set down on an electric *per se*.

3. The phial will be electrified as strongly, if held by the hook, and the coating apply'd to the globe or tube; as when held by the coating, and the hook apply'd.[1]

4. But the *direction* of the electrical fire, being different in the charging, will also be different in the explosion. The bottle charged through the hook, will be discharged through the hook; the bottle charged through the coating, will be discharged through the coating; and not otherways; for the fire must come out the same way it went in.

---

[1] This was a Discovery of the very ingenious Mr. *Kinnersley's*, and by him communicated to me.

5. To prove this, take two bottles that were equally charged through the hooks, one in each hand; bring their hooks near each other, and no spark or shock will follow; because each hook is disposed to give fire, and neither to receive it. Set one of the bottles down on glass, take it up by the hook, and apply its coating to the hook of the other; then there will be an explosion and shock, and both bottles will be discharged.

6. Vary the experiment, by charging two phials equally, one through the hook, the other through the coating; hold that by the coating which was charged through the hook; and that by the hook which was charged through the coating; apply the hook of the first to the coating of the other, and there will be no shock or spark. Set that down on glass which you held by the hook, take it up by the coating, and bring the two hooks together: a spark and shock will follow, and both phials be discharged.

In this experiment the bottles are totally discharged, or the equilibrium within them restored. The *abounding* of fire in one of the hooks (or rather in the internal surface of one bottle) being exactly equal to the *wanting* of the other; and therefore, as each bottle has in itself the *abounding* as well as the *wanting*, the wanting and abounding must be equal in each bottle. See § 8, 9, 10, 11. But if a man holds in his hands two bottles, one fully electrified, the other not at all, and brings their hooks together, he has but half a shock, and the bottles will both remain half electrified, the one being half discharged, and the other half charged.

7. Place two phials equally charged on a table, at five or six inches distance. Let a cork ball, suspended by a silk thread, hang between them. If the phials were both charged through their hooks, the cork, when it has been attracted and repelled by the one, will not be attracted, but equally repelled by the other. But, if the phials were charged, the one through the hook, and the other through the coating,[1] the ball, when it is repelled from one hook, will be as strongly attracted by the

---

[1] To charge a bottle commodiously through the coating, place it on a glass stand; form a communication from the prime conductor to the coating, and another from the hook to the wall or floor. When it is charged, remove the latter communication before you take hold of the bottle, otherwise great part of the fire will escape by it.

other, and play vigorously between them [fetching the electric fluid from the one, and delivering it to the other—1774] till both phials are nearly discharged.

8. When we use the terms of *charging* and *discharging* the phial, it is in compliance with custom, and for want of others more suitable. Since we are of opinion, that there is really no more electrical fire in the phial after what is called its *charging*, than before, nor less after its *discharging*; excepting only the small spark that might be given to, and taken from, the non-electric matter, if separated from the bottle, which spark may not be equal to a five-hundredth part of what is called the explosion.

For if, on the explosion, the electrical fire came out of the bottle by one part, and did not enter in again by another, then, if a man, standing on wax, and holding the bottle in one hand, takes the spark by touching the wire hook with the other, the bottle being thereby *discharged*, the man would be *charged;* or whatever fire was lost by one, would be found in the other, since there was no way for its escape: But the contrary is true.

9. Besides, the phial will not suffer what is called a *charging*, unless as much fire can go out of it one way, as is thrown in by another. A phial cannot be charged standing on wax or glass, or hanging on the prime conductor, unless a communication be formed between its coating and the floor.

10. But suspend two or more phials on the prime conductor, one hanging to the tail of the other; and a wire from the last to the floor, an equal number of turns of the wheel shall charge them all equally, and every one as much as one alone would have been; what is driven out at the tail of the first, serving to charge the second; what is driven out of the second charging the third; and so on. By this means a great number of bottles might be charged with the same labour, and equally high, with one alone, were it not that every bottle receives new fire, and loses its old with some reluctance, or rather gives some small resistance to the charging, which in a number of bottles becomes more equal to the charging power, and so repels the fire back again on the globe, sooner [in proportion] than a single bottle would do.

11. When a bottle is charged in the common way, its *inside* and *outside surfaces* stand ready, the one to give fire by the hook, the other to receive it by the coating; the one is full, and ready to throw out, the other empty and extremely hungry; yet as the first will not *give out*, unless the other can at the same instant *receive in*, so neither will the latter receive in, unless the first can at the same instant give out. When both can be done at once, it is done with inconceivable quickness and violence.

12. So a strait spring (though the comparison does not agree in every particular) when forcibly bent, must, to restore itself, contract that side which in the bending was extended, and extend that which was contracted; if either of these two operations be hindered, the other cannot be done. But the spring is not said to be *charg'd* with elasticity when bent, and *discharged* when unbent; its quantity of elasticity is always the same.

13. Glass, in like manner, has within its substance always the same quantity of electrical fire, and that a very great quantity in proportion to the mass of glass, as shall be shewn hereafter.

14. This quantity, proportioned to the glass, it strongly and obstinately retains, and will have neither more nor less though it will suffer a change to be made in its parts and situation; that is, we may take away part of it from one of the sides, provided we throw an equal quantity into the other.

15. Yet, when the situation of the electrical fire is thus altered in the glass; when some has been taken from one side, and some added to the other, it will not be at rest, or in its natural state, till it is restored to its original equality. And this restitution cannot be made through the substance of the glass, but must be done by a non-electric communication formed without, from surface to surface.

16. Thus, the whole force of the bottle, and power of giving a shock, is in the *glass itself;* the non-electrics in contact with the two surfaces, serving only to *give* and *receive* to and from the several parts of the glass; that is, to give on one side, and take away from the other.

17. This was discovered here in the following manner: Purposing to analyze the electrified bottle, in order to find wherein its strength

lay, we placed it on glass, and drew out the cork and wire, which for that purpose had been loosely put in. Then taking the bottle in one hand, and bringing a finger of the other near its mouth, a strong spark came from the water, and the shock was as violent as if the wire had remained in it, which shewed that the force did not lie in the wire. Then, to find if it resided in the water, being crouded into and condensed in it, as confin'd by the glass, which had been our former opinion, we electrified the bottle again, and, placing it on glass, drew out the wire and cork as before; then, taking up the bottle, we decanted all its water into an empty bottle, which likewise stood on glass; and taking up that other bottle, we expected, if the force resided in the water, to find a shock from it; but there was none. We judged then, that it must either be lost in decanting, or remain in the first bottle. The latter we found to be true; for that bottle on trial gave the shock, though filled up as it stood with fresh unelectrified water from a tea-pot. To find, then, whether glass had this property merely as glass, or whether the form contributed any thing to it; we took a pane of sash-glass, and, laying it on the hand [stand], placed a plate of lead on its upper surface; then electrified that plate, and bringing a finger to it, there was a spark and shock. We then took two plates of lead of equal dimensions, but less than the glass by two inches every way, and electrified the glass between them, by electrifying the uppermost lead; then separated the glass from the lead, in doing which, what little fire might be in the lead was taken out, and the glass being touched in the electrified parts with a finger, afforded only very small pricking sparks, but a great number of them might be taken from different places. Then dexterously placing it again between the leaden plates, and compleating a circle between the two surfaces, a violent shock ensued. Which demonstrated the power to reside in glass as glass, and that the non-electrics in contact served only, like the armature of a loadstone, to unite the force of the several parts, and bring them at once to any point desired; it being the property of a non-electric, that the whole body instantly receives or gives what electrical fire is given to, or taken from, any one of its parts.

18. Upon this we made what we called an *electrical battery*, con-

sisting of eleven panes of large sash-glass, arm'd with thin leaden plates, pasted on each side, placed vertically, and supported at two inches distance on silk cords, with thick hooks of leaden wire, one from each side, standing upright, distant from each other, and convenient communications of wire and chain, from the giving side of one pane, to the receiving side of the other; that so the whole might be charged together, and with the same labour as one single pane; and another contrivance to bring the giving sides, after charging, in contact with one long wire, and the receivers with another, which two long wires would give the force of all the plates of glass at once through the body of any animal forming the circle with them. The plates may also be discharged separately, or any number together that is required. But this machine is not much used, as not perfectly answering our intention with regard to the ease of charging, for the reason given, *Sec.* 10. We made also, of large glass panes, magical pictures, and self-moving animated wheels, presently to be described.

19. I perceive by the ingenious Mr. *Watson's* last book, lately received, that Dr. *Bevis* had used, before we had, panes of glass to give a shock;[1] though till that book came to hand, I thought to have communicated it to you as a novelty. The excuse for mentioning it here is, that we tried the experiment differently, drew different consequences from it (for Mr. *Watson* still seems to think the fire *accumulated on the non-electric* that is in contact with the glass, p. 72) and, as far as we hitherto know, have carried it farther.

20. The magical picture[2] is made thus. Having a large metzotinto with a frame and glass, suppose of the KING, (God preserve him) take out the print, and cut a pannel out of it near two inches distant from the frame all round. If the cut is through the picture, it is not the worse. With thin paste, or gum-water, fix the border that is cut off on the inside the glass, pressing it smooth and close; then fill up the vacancy by gilding the glass well with leaf-gold, or brass. Gild likewise the inner edge of the back of the frame all round, except the top part,

---

[1] I have since heard, that Mr. *Smeaton* was the first who made use of panes of glass for that purpose.

[2] Contrived by Mr. *Kinnersley*.

and form a communication between that gilding and the gilding behind the glass: then put in the board, and that side is finished. Turn up the glass, and gild the fore side exactly over the back gilding, and when it is dry, cover it by pasting on the pannel of the picture that hath been cut out, observing to bring the correspondent parts of the border and picture together, by which the picture will appear of a piece, as at first, only part is behind the glass, and part before. Hold the picture horizontally by the top, and place a little moveable gilt crown on the king's head. If now the picture be moderately electrified, and another person take hold of the frame with one hand, so that his fingers touch its inside gilding, and with the other hand endeavour to take off the crown, he will receive a terrible blow, and fail in the attempt. If the picture were highly charged, the consequence might perhaps be as fatal[1] as that of high treason, for when the spark is taken through a quire of paper laid on the picture, by means of a wire communication, it makes a fair hole through every sheet, that is, through forty-eight leaves, though a quire of paper is thought good armour against the push of a sword, or even against a pistol bullet, and the crack is exceeding loud. The operator, who holds the picture by the upper end, where the inside of the frame is not gilt, to prevent its falling, feels nothing of the shock, and may touch the face of the picture without danger, which he pretends is a test of his loyalty. If a ring of persons take the shock among them, the experiment is called *The Conspirators.*

21. On the principle, in *Sec.* 7, that hooks of bottles, differently charged, will attract and repel differently, is made an electrical wheel, that turns with considerable strength. A small upright shaft of wood passes at right angles through a thin round board, of about twelve inches diameter, and turns on a sharp point of iron, fixed in the lower end, while a strong wire in the upper end, passing through a small hole in a thin brass plate, keeps the shaft truly vertical. About thirty *radii* of equal length, made of sash-glass, cut in narrow strips, issue

---

[1] We have since found it fatal to small animals, though not to large ones. The biggest we have yet killed is a hen. 1750.

horizontally from the circumference of the board, the ends most distant from the center being about four inches apart. On the end of every one, a brass thimble is fixed. If now the wire of a bottle electrified in the common way, be brought near the circumference of this wheel, it will attract the nearest thimble, and so put the wheel in motion; that thimble, in passing by, receives a spark, and thereby being electrified is repelled, and so driven forwards; while a second being attracted, approaches the wire, receives a spark, and is driven after the first, and so on till the wheel has gone once round, when the thimbles before electrified approaching the wire, instead of being attracted as they were at first, are repelled, and the motion presently ceases. But if another bottle, which had been charged through the coating, be placed near the same wheel, its wire will attract the thimble repelled by the first, and thereby double the force that carries the wheel round; and not only taking out the fire that had been communicated to the thimbles by the first bottle, but even robbing them of their natural quantity, instead of being repelled when they come again towards the first bottle, they are more strongly attracted, so that the wheel mends its pace, till it goes with great rapidity, twelve or fifteen rounds in a minute, and with such strength, as that the weight of one hundred *Spanish* dollars, with which we once loaded it, did not seem in the least to retard its motion. This is called an electrical jack; and if a large fowl were spitted on the upright shaft, it would be carried round before a fire with a motion fit for roasting.

22. But this wheel, like those driven by wind, water, or weights, moves by a foreign force, to wit, that of the bottles. The self-moving wheel, though constructed on the same principles, appears more surprising. 'Tis made of a thin round plate of window-glass, seventeen inches diameter, well gilt on both sides, all but two inches next the edge. Two small hemispheres of wood are then fixed with cement to the middle of the upper and under sides, centrally opposite, and in each of them a thick strong wire eight or ten inches long, which together make the axis of the wheel. It turns horizontally on a point at the lower end of its axis, which rests on a bit of brass cemented within a glass salt-cellar. The upper end of its axis passes through a hole in a

thin brass plate cemented to a long strong piece of glass, which keeps it six or eight inches distant from any non-electric, and has a small ball of wax or metal on its top, to keep in the fire. In a circle on the table which supports the wheel, are fixed twelve small pillars of glass, at about four inches distance, with a thimble on the top of each. On the edge of the wheel is a small leaden bullet, communicating by a wire with the gilding of the *upper* surface of the wheel; and about six inches from it is another bullet communicating in like manner with the *under* surface. When the wheel is to be charged by the upper surface, a communication must be made from the under surface to the table. When it is well charged, it begins to move; the bullet nearest to a pillar moves towards the thimble on that pillar, and passing by, electrifies it, and then pushes itself from it; the succeeding bullet, which communicates with the other surface of the glass, more strongly attracts that thimble, on account of its being before electrified by the other bullet; and thus the wheel increases its motion till it comes to such a height that the resistance of the air regulates it. It will go half an hour, and make one minute with another twenty turns in a minute, which is six hundred turns in the whole; the bullet of the upper surface giving in each turn twelve sparks, to the thimbles, which makes seven thousand two hundred sparks; and the bullet of the under surface receiving as many from the thimbles; those bullets moving in the time near two thousand five hundred feet. The thimbles are well fixed, and in so exact a circle, that the bullets may pass within a very small distance of each of them. If, instead of two bullets you put eight, four communicating with the upper surface, and four with the under surface, placed alternately; which eight, at about six inches distance, completes the circumference, the force and swiftness will be greatly increased, the wheel making fifty turns in a minute; but then it will not continue moving so long. These wheels may be applied, perhaps, to the ringing of chimes,[1] and moving of light-made orreries.

23. A small wire bent circularly, with a loop at each end; let one

---

[1] This was afterwards done with success by Mr. *Kinnersley*.

end rest against the under surface of the wheel, and bring the other end near the upper surface, it will give a terrible crack, and the force will be discharged.

24. Every spark in that manner drawn from the surface of the wheel, makes a round hole in the gilding, tearing off a part of it in coming out; which shews that the fire is not accumulated on the gilding, but is in the glass itself.

25. The gilding being varnished over with turpentine varnish, the varnish, though dry and hard, is burnt by the spark drawn through it, and gives a strong smell and visible smoke. And when the spark is drawn through paper, all round the hole made by it, the paper will be blacked by the smoke, which sometimes penetrates several of the leaves. Part of the gilding torn off, is also found forcibly driven into the hole made in the paper by the stroke.

26. It is amazing to observe in how small a portion of glass a great electrical force may lie. A thin glass bubble, about an inch diameter, weighing only six grains, being half filled with water, partly gilt on the outside, and furnish'd with a wire hook, gives, when electrified, as great a shock as a man can well bear. As the glass is thickest near the orifice, I suppose the lower half, which being gilt was electrified and gave the shock, did not exceed two grains; for it appeared, when broke, much thinner than the upper half. If one of these thin bottles be electrified by the coating, and the spark taken out through the gilding, it will break the glass inwards, at the same time that it breaks the gilding outwards.

27. And allowing (for the reasons before given, §. 8, 9, 10,) that there is no more electrical fire in a bottle after charging than before, how great must be the quantity in this small portion of glass! It seems as if it were of its very substance and essence. Perhaps if that due quantity of electrical fire so obstinately retained by glass, could be separated from it, it would no longer be glass; it might lose its transparency, or its brittleness, or its elasticity. Experiments may possibly be invented hereafter to discover this.

28. We were surprised at the account given in Mr. *Watson's* book, of a shock communicated through a great space of dry ground, and

suspect there must be some metalline quality in the gravel of that ground; having found that simple dry earth, rammed in a glass tube, open at both ends, and a wire hook inserted in the earth at each end, the earth and wires making part of a circuit, would not conduct the least perceptible shock, and indeed when one wire was electrified, the other hardly shewed any signs of its being in connection with it.[1] Even a thoroughly wet packthread sometimes fails of conducting a shock, though it otherwise conducts Electricity very well. A dry cake of ice, or an icicle held between two in a circle, likewise prevents the shock, which one would not expect, as water conducts it so perfectly well. Gilding on a new book, though at first it conducts the shock extremely well, yet fails after ten or a dozen experiments, though it appears otherwise in all respects the same, which we cannot account for.[2]

29. There is one experiment more which surprizes us, and is not hitherto satisfactorily accounted for; it is this: Place an iron shot on a glass stand, and let a ball of damp cork, suspended by a silk thread, hang in contact with the shot. Take a bottle in each hand, one that is electrified through the hook, the other through the coating: Apply the giving wire to the shot, which will electrify it *positively*, and the cork shall be repelled: then apply the requiring wire, which will take out the spark given by the other; when the cork will return to the shot: Apply the same again, and take out another spark, so will the shot be electrified *negatively*, and the cork in that case shall be repelled equally as before. Then apply the giving wire to the shot, and give the spark it wanted, so will the cork return: Give it another, which will be an addition to its natural quantity, so will the cork be repelled again: And so may the experiment be repeated as long as there is any charge in the bottles. Which shews, that bodies having less than

---

[1] Probably the ground is never so dry.

[2] We afterwards found that it failed after one stroke with a large bottle; and the continuity of the gold appearing broken, and many of its parts dissipated, the Electricity could not pass the remaining parts without leaping from part to part through the air, which always resists the motion of this fluid, and was probably the cause of the gold's not conducting so well as before.

the common quantity of Electricity, repel each other, as well as those that have more.

Chagrined a little that we have been hitherto able to produce nothing in this way of use to mankind; and the hot weather coming on, when electrical experiments are not so agreeable, it is proposed to put an end to them for this season, somewhat humorously, in a party of pleasure on the banks of *Skuylkil*.[1] Spirits, at the same time, are to be fired by a spark sent from side to side through the river, without any other conductor than the water; an experiment which we some time since performed, to the amazement of many.[2] A turkey is to be killed for our dinner by the *electrical shock*, and roasted by the *electrical jack*, before a fire kindled by the *electrified bottle:* when the healths of all the famous electricians in *England, Holland, France,* and *Germany* are to be drank in *electrified bumpers*,[3] under the discharge of guns from the *electrical battery.*

---

[1] The river that washes one side of *Philadelphia* as the *Delaware* does the other; both are ornamented with the summer habitations of the citizens, and the agreeable mansions of the principal people of this colony.

[2] As the possibility of this experiment has not been easily conceived, I shall here describe it. Two iron rods, about three feet long, were planted just within the margin of the river, on the opposite sides. A thick piece of wire, with a small round knob at its end, was fixed to the top of one of the rods, bending downwards, so as to deliver commodiously the spark upon the surface of the spirit. A small wire fastened by one end to the handle of the spoon, containing the spirit, was carried across the river, and supported in the air by the rope commonly used to hold by, in drawing the ferry-boats over. The other end of this wire was tied round the coating of the bottle; which being charged, the spark was delivered from the hook to the top of the rod standing in the water on that side. At the same instant the rod on the other side delivered a spark into the spoon, and fired the spirit; the electric fire returning to the coating of the bottle, through the handle of the spoon and the supported wire connected with them.

That the electric fire thus actually passes through the water, has since been satisfactorily demonstrated to many by an experiment of Mr. *Kinnersley's*, performed in a trough of water about ten feet long. The hand being placed under water in the direction of the spark (which always takes the strait or shortest course) is struck and penetrated by it as it passes.

[3] An *electrified bumper* is a small thin glass tumbler, near filled with wine, and electrified as the bottle. This when brought to the lips gives a shock, if the party be close shaved, and does not breathe on the liquor.

To PETER COLLINSON. *September 27, 1750*

Additional Experiment

Additional Experiment proving that the Leyden Bottle has no more Electrical Fire in it, when charg'd, than before; nor less when discharg'd. That in Discharging, the Fire does not issue from the Wire and Coating at the same Time, as some have thought; but that the Coating always receives what is discharg'd by the Wire, or an equal Quantity: the outer Surface being always in a negative State of Electricity, when the inner Surface is in a positive State.

Place a thick Plate of Glass under the rubbing Cushion, to cut off the Communication of Electrical Fire from the Floor to the Cushion: Then if there be no fine Points or hairy Threads Sticking out from the Cushion or from the Parts of the Machine opposite to the Cushion, of which you must be careful, you can get but a few Sparks from the Prime Conductor; which are all the Cushion will part with.

Hang a Vial then on the Prime Conductor, and it will not charge, tho' you hold it by the Coating. But

Form a Communication by a Chain from the Coating to the Cushion, and the Phial will charge.

For the Globe then draws the Electrical Fire out of the Outside Surface of the Phial and forces it thro' the Prime Conductor and Wire of the Phial into the inside Surface.

Thus the Bottle is charg'd with it's own Fire, no other being to be had, while the Glass Plate is under the Cushion.

Hang two Cork Balls by Flaxen Threads to the Prime Conductor, then touch the Coating of the Bottle, and they will be electrified, and recede from each other.

For just as much Fire as you give the Coating, so much is discharg'd thro' the Wire upon the Prime Conductor, whence the Cork Balls receive an Electrical Atmosphere. But

Take a Wire bent in this Form with a Wax Handle to hold it by, and apply one End of this Wire to the Coating and the other at the Same Time to the Prime Conductor; the Vial will be discharged. And if the Balls are not electrified before the Discharge, neither will they appear to be so after the Discharge, for they will not repel each other.

Now if the Fire, discharg'd from the inside Surface of the Bottle, thro' its Wire, remain'd on the prime Conductor, the Balls would be electrified and recede from each other.

If the Vial really exploded at both Ends and discharged Fire from both Coating and Wire, the Balls would be more electrified and recede farther: for none of the Fire can escape, the Wax Handle preventing.

But if the Fire with which the inside Surface is surcharg'd be so much precisely as is wanted by the outside Surface, it will pass round thro' the Wire fixt to the Wax Handle, restore the Equilibrium in the Glass and make no Alteration in the State of the Prime Conductor.

Accordingly we find that if the Prime Conductor be electrified, and the Cork Balls in a State of Repellancy, before the Bottle is discharg'd, they continue so afterwards: If not, they are not electrified by that Discharge.

To JOHN FRANKLIN. *25 December, 1750*

I have lately made an experiment in electricity, that I desire never to repeat. Two nights ago, being about to kill a turkey by the shock from two large glass jars, containing as much electrical fire as forty common phials, I inadvertently took the whole through my own arms and body, by receiving the fire from the united top wires with one hand, while the other held a chain connected with the outsides of both jars. The company present (whose talking to me, and to one another, I suppose occasioned my inattention to what I was about) say, that the flash was very great, and the crack as loud as a pistol; yet, my senses being instantly gone, I neither saw the one nor heard the other; nor did I feel the stroke on my hand, though I afterwards found it raised a round swelling where the fire entered, as big as half a pistol-bullet; by which you may judge of the quickness of the electrical fire, which by this instance seems to be greater than that of sound, light, or animal sensation.

What I can remember of the matter is that I was about to try whether the bottles or jars were fully charged, by the strength and length of the stream issuing to my hand, as I commonly used to do, and which I might safely enough have done if I had not held the chain in the other hand. I then felt what I know not how well to describe; a universal blow throughout my whole body from head to foot, which seemed within as well as without; after which the first thing I took notice of was a violent quick shaking of my body, which gradually remitting, my sense as gradually returned, and then I thought the bottles must be discharged, but could not conceive how, till at last I perceived the chain in my hand, and recollected what I had been about to do. That part of my hand and fingers, which held the chain, was left white, as though the blood had been driven out, and remained so eight or ten minutes after, feeling like dead flesh; and I had a numbness in my arms and the back of my neck, which continued till the next morning, but wore off. Nothing remains now of this shock, but a soreness in my breast-bone, which feels as if it had been bruised. I did not fall, but suppose I should have been knocked down, if I had received the stroke in my head. The whole was over in less than a minute.

You may communicate this to Mr. Bowdoin, as a caution to him, but do not make it more public, for I am ashamed to have been guilty of so notorious a blunder; a match for that of the Irishman, whom my sister told me of, who, to divert his wife, poured the bottle of gunpowder on the live coal; or of that other, who, being about to steal powder, made a hole in the cask with a hot iron. I am yours, &c.

P. S. The jars hold six gallons each.

To PETER COLLINSON. *February 4, 1750*

By Ouchterlony I sent you my last Piece on Electricity, and have nothing new to add, except that Mr. Kinnersley, an ingenious Gentleman of this Place has apply'd my horizontal self-moving Wheel with Success, to the playing of Tunes on Chimes, which it does very prettily. I will get Mr. Evans to make a Draft of his Machine, and send it to you.

My Respects to Mr. Watson. He desir'd you to enquire what Success we had in our Attempts to kill a Turkey by the Electrical Strokes. Please to acquaint him, that we made several Experiments on Fowls this Winter; That we found two large thin glass Jars, gilt (holding each about 6 Gallons, and taking 2000 Turns of a Globe of 9 Inches Diameter to charge them full, when the Globe works very well, and will charge a common half pint Vial with 50 Turns) were sufficient to kill common Hens outright; but the Turkies, tho' thrown into violent Convulsions, and then lying as dead for some Minutes, would recover in less than a quarter of an Hour. However, having added Mr. Kinnersley's Jarrs and mine together, in all 5, tho' not fully charg'd, we kill'd a Turky with them of about 10 lb.wt. and suppose they would have kill'd a much larger. I conceit that the Birds kill'd in this Manner eat uncommonly tender.

In making these Experiments, I found that a Man can without great Detriment bear a much greater Electrical Shock than I imagin'd. For I inadvertently took the Stroke of two of those Jars thro' my Arms and Body, when they were very near full charg'd. It seem'd an universal Blow from head to foot throughout the Body, and was follow'd by a violent quick Trembling in the Trunk, which wore gradually off in a few seconds. It was some Moments before I could collect my Thoughts so as to know what was the Matter; for I did not see the Flash tho' my Eye was on the Spot of the Prime Conductor from whence it struck the Back of my Hand, nor did I hear the Crack tho' the By-standers say it was a loud one; nor did I particularly feel the Stroke on my Hand, tho' I afterwards found it had rais'd a Swelling there the bigness of half a Swan Shot or pistol Bullet. My Arms and Back of my Neck felt somewhat numb the remainder of the Evening, and my Breastbone was sore for a Week after, [as] if it had been bruiz'd. What the Consequence would be, if such a Shock were taken thro' the Head, I know not.

All the Instruments by Shirley, &c. and Books for the Academy came safe. Also those for the Library mention'd in your Letters.

Our Friend Mr. Kalm, goes home in this Ship, with a great Cargo of Curious Things. I love the Man, and admire his indefatigable Industry. I shall do my best Endeavour to have [the] Study of Natural History establish'd in the Academy, as what [I] am convinc'd is a Science of more real Worth and Usefulness, [than] several of the others we propose to teach, put together.

(c) Quantitative Outlook

In his March 18, 1755, letter to John Lining (p. 102), Franklin noted that a cork suspended in an electrified silver can was neither attracted nor repelled by it (cf. Faraday's celebrated ice-pail experiment in 1843). Repeating this experiment in 1766, Priestley inferred the existence of an inverse-square law of force between relatively small electrified bodies. At the same time he pointed out the need for good measuring instruments—not available before 1760. The Scotch physicist John Robison (1739–1805) confirmed this law approximately by experiment in 1769. Meanwhile the English astronomer and geologist John Michell (1724–93) had suggested the use of a balance for making precise measurements of such forces. The French military engineer Charles Augustin de Coulomb (1736–1806) used a torsion balance and thus determined the fundamental law of force between electrostatic charges (like charges in 1785, unlike ones in 1787). (The physicist and chemist Henry Cavendish had made similar investigations in 1779 but they were not published until a century later by the Scottish physicist James Clerk Maxwell (1831–79).) The determination of this law together with the principle of conservation of electric charge established electrostatics as a so-called "exact" science—in so far as any science can be said to be exact.

(d) Franklin Experiment

It was natural to compare superficially lightning with electric sparks and to speculate about their possible relation; it had been done by Havksbee (1705), William Wall (1708), Newton (1716), Johann Heinrich Winkler (1746), John Freke (1746), and Nollet (1748). Gray, indeed, had remarked in 1734, "Electric fire seems to be of the same nature with that of thunder and lightning." Franklin himself wrote in 1747, "We represent lightning, by passing the wire in the dark over a china plate that has gift flowers." What was needed was a critical experiment that would unquestionably identify the two. One of Franklin's significant contributions was the design of such an experiment.

In his letter of May 25, 1747, he mentioned "the wonderful effect of points;" on March 2, 1750, he mused, "The doctrine of points is very curious."

The whole electrification of a conductor always lies on its surface; its surface density depends upon the shape of the conductor being greatest for points. The intensity of the outward electric force may become so high as to make the surrounding air lose its insulating power and become conducting—there will then be a discharge, e.g. an electric spark.

Even today, after many investigations, details of the phenomena of discharge, with the associated conduction of electricity in gases under various physical conditions, are still far from being quite understood quantitatively.

Later, Franklin told Lining about the comparison he had made of the properties of electric sparks and lightning which he had recorded in his notebook in 1749 with the injunction, "Let the experiment be made!"

His actual suggestion of drawing lightning (strictly speaking, an induced effect) from an electrified cloud to a pointed metal rod is described in an enclosure on *"Opinions and conjectures concerning the properties and effects of the electrical matter, arising from experiments and observations made in Philadelphia in 1749"*, which he sent in a letter to Collinson July 29, 1750. Some members of the Royal Society are said to have laughed at the suggestion of such action by lightning and a point; at any rate it was not published in the *Transactions*.

The notice of his own kite experiment was published in the October 19, 1752, issue of the *Pennsylvania Gazette*. Priestley's account was given in his *History and Present State of Electricity* (1769) (ref. 6, pp. 171–172).

To John Lining. *March 18, 1755*

Your question, how I came first to think of proposing the experiment of drawing down the lightning, in order to ascertain its sameness with the electric fluid, I cannot answer better than by giving you an extract from the minutes I used to keep of the experiments I made, with memorandums of such as I purposed to make, the reasons for making them, and the observations that arose upon them, from which minutes my letters were afterwards drawn. By this extract you will see, that the thought was not so much "an out-of-the-way one," but that it might have occurred to any electrician.

"*November* 7, 1749. Electrical fluid agrees with lightning in these particulars. 1. Giving light. 2. Colour of the light. 3. Crooked direction. 4. Swift motion. 5. Being conducted by metals. 6. Crack or noise in exploding. 7. Subsisting in water or ice. 8. Rending bodies it passes through. 9. Destroying animals. 10. Melting metals. 11. Firing inflammable substances. 12. Sulphureous smell. The electric fluid is attracted by points. We do not know whether this property is in lightning. But since they agree in all particulars wherein we can already compare them, is it not probable they agree likewise in this? Let the experiment be made."

I wish I could give you any satisfaction in the article of clouds. I am still at a loss about the manner in which they become charged with

Electricity; no hypothesis I have yet formed perfectly satisfying me. Some time since, I heated very hot a brass plate, two feet square, and placed it on an electric stand. From the plate a wire extended horizontally four or five feet, and, at the end of it, hung, by linnen-threads, a pair of cork balls. I then repeatedly sprinkled water over the plate, that it might be raised from it in vapour, hoping that if the vapour either carried off the electricity of the plate, or left behind it that of the water, (one of which I supposed it must do, if, like the clouds, it became electrised itself, either positively or negatively) I should perceive and determine it by the separation of the balls, and by finding whether they were positive or negative; but no alteration was made at all, nor could I perceive that the steam was itself electrised, though I have still some suspicion that the steam was not fully examined, and I think the experiment should be repeated. Whether the first state of electrised clouds is positive or negative, if I could find the cause of that, I should be at no loss about the other, for either is easily deduced from the other, as one state is easily produced by the other. A strongly positive cloud may drive out of a neighbouring cloud much of its natural quantity of the electric fluid, and, passing by it, leave it in a negative state. In the same way, a strongly negative cloud may occasion a neighbouring cloud to draw into itself from others an additional quantity, and, passing by it, leave it in a positive state. How these effects may be produced, you will easily conceive, on perusing and considering the experiments in the enclosed paper: And from them too it appears probable, that every change from positive to negative, and from negative to positive, that, during a thunder gust, we see in the cork-balls annexed to the apparatus, is not owing to the presence of clouds in the same state, but often to the absence of positive or negative clouds, that, having just passed, leave the rod in the opposite state.

The knocking down of the six men was performed with two of my large jarrs not fully charged. I laid one end of my discharging rod upon the head of the first; he laid his hand on the head of the second; the second his hand on the head of the third, and so to the last, who held, in his hand, the chain that was connected with the outside of the jarrs. When they were thus placed, I applied the other end of my rod to the prime-conductor, and they all dropt together. When they got up, they all declared they had not felt any stroke, and wondered how they came to fall; nor did any of them either hear the crack, or see the light of it. You suppose it a dangerous experiment; but I had once suffered the same myself, receiving, by accident, an equal stroke through my head, that struck me down, without hurting me: And I had seen a young woman, that was about to be electrified through the feet, (for some indisposition) receive a greater charge through the head, by inadvertently stooping forward to look at the placing of her feet, till her forehead (as she was very tall) came too near my prime-conductor: She dropt, but instantly got up again, complaining of nothing. A person so struck, sinks down doubled, or folded together as it were, the joints losing their strength and stiffness at once, so that he drops on the spot where he stood, instantly, and there is no previous staggering, nor does he ever fall lengthwise. Too great a charge might, indeed, kill a man, but I have not yet seen any hurt done by it. It would certainly, as you observe, be the easiest of all deaths.

The experiment you have heard so imperfect an account of, is merely this.—I electrified a silver pint cann, on an electric stand, and then lowered into it a cork ball, of about an inch diameter, hanging by a silk string, till the cork touched the bottom of the cann. The cork was not attracted to the inside of the cann, as it would have been to the outside, and though it touched the bottom, yet, when drawn out, it was not found to be electrified by that touch, as it would have been by touching the outside. The fact is singular. You require the reason; I do not know it. Perhaps you may discover it, and then you will be so good as to communicate it to me.[1] I find a frank acknowledgement of one's ignorance is not only the easiest way to get rid of a difficulty, but the likeliest way to obtain information, and therefore I practise it: I think it an honest policy. Those who affect to be thought to know

---

[1] Mr. *F.* has since thought, that, possibly, the mutual repulsion of the inner opposite sides of the electrified cann, may prevent the accumulating an electric atmosphere upon them, and occasion it to stand chiefly on the outside. But recommends it to the farther examination of the curious.

every thing, and so undertake to explain every thing, often remain long ignorant of many things that others could and would instruct them in, if they appeared less conceited.

The treatment your friend has met with is so common, that no man who knows what the world is, and ever has been, should expect to escape it. There are every where a number of people, who, being totally destitute of any inventive faculty themselves, do not readily conceive that others may possess it: They think of inventions as of miracles; there might be such formerly, but they are ceased. With these, every one who offers a new invention is deem'd a pretender: He had it from some other country, or from some book: A man of *their own acquaintance;* one who has no more sense than themselves, could not possibly, in their opinion, have been the inventer of any thing. They are confirmed, too, in these sentiments, by frequent instances of pretensions to invention, which vanity is daily producing. That vanity too, though an incitement to invention, is, at the same time, the pest of inventors. Jealousy and Envy deny the merit or the novelty of your invention; but Vanity, when the novelty and merit are established, claims it for its own. The smaller your invention is, the more mortification you receive in having the credit of it disputed with you by a rival, whom the jealousy and envy of others are ready to support against you, at least so far as to make the point doubtful. It is not in itself of importance enough for a dispute; no one would think your proofs and reasons worth their attention: And yet if you do not dispute the point, and demonstrate your right, you not only lose the credit of being in that instance *ingenious*, but you suffer the disgrace of not being *ingenuous;* not only of being a plagiary, but of being a plagiary for trifles. Had the invention been greater it would have disgrac'd you less; for men have not so contemptible an idea of him that robs for gold on the highway, as of him that can pick pockets for half-pence and farthings. Thus, through Envy, Jealousy, and the Vanity of competitors for Fame, the origin of many of the most extraordinary inventions, though produced within but a few centuries past, is involved in doubt and uncertainty. We scarce know to whom we are indebted for the *compass*, and for *spectacles*, nor have even *paper* and *printing*, that record every thing else, been able to preserve with certainty the name and reputation of their inventors. One would not, therefore, of all faculties or qualities of the mind, wish, for a friend, or a child, that he should have that of invention. For his attempts to benefit mankind in that way, however well imagined, if they do not succeed, expose him, though very unjustly, to general ridicule and contempt; and, if they do succeed, to envy, robbery, and abuse.

To PETER COLLINSON. *July 29, 1750*

As you first put us on electrical experiments, by sending to our library company a tube, with directions how to use it; and as our honourable proprietary enabled us to carry those experiments to a greater height, by his generous present of a compleat electrical apparatus; 'tis fit that both should know, from time to time, what progress we make. It was in this view I wrote and sent you my former papers on this subject, desiring, that, as I had not the honour of a direct correspondence with that bountiful benefactor to our library, they might be communicated to him through your hands. In the same view I write and send you this additional paper. If it happens to bring you nothing new, (which may well be, considering the number of ingenious men in *Europe*, continually engaged in the same researches) at least it will show, that the instruments put into our hands are not neglected; and, that if no valuable discoveries are made by us, whatever the cause may be, it is not want of industry and application.

Opinions and Conjectures, concerning the Properties and Effects of the Electrical Matter, arising from Experiments and Observations, made at Philadelphia, 1749.

§ 1. THE electrical matter consists of particles extremely subtile, since it can permeate common matter, even the densest metals, with such ease and freedom as not to receive any perceptible resistance.

2. If any one should doubt whether the electrical matter passes thro' the substance of bodies, or only over and along their surfaces, a shock from an electrified large glass jar, taken through his own body, will probably convince him.

3. Electrical matter differs from common matter in this, that the parts of the latter mutually attract, those of the former mutually repel, each other. Hence the appearing divergency in a stream of electrified effluvia.

4. But though the particles of electrical matter do repel each other, they are strongly attracted by all other matter.[1]

5. From these three things, the extreme subtilty of the electrical matter, the mutual repulsion of its parts, and the strong attraction between them and other matter, arise this effect, that, when a quantity of electrical matter is applied to a mass of common matter, of any bigness or length, within our observation, (which hath not already got its quantity) it is immediately and equally diffused through the whole.

6. Thus, common matter is a kind of spunge to the electrical fluid. And as a spunge would receive no water if the parts of water were not smaller than the pores of the spunge; and even then but slowly, if there were not a mutual attraction between those parts and the parts of the spunge; and would still imbibe it faster, if the mutual attraction among the parts of the water did not impede, some force being required to separate them; and fastest, if, instead of attraction, there were a mutual repulsion among those parts, which would act in conjuction with the attraction of the spunge; so is the case between the electrical and common matter.

7. But in common matter there is (generally) as much of the electrical, as it will contain within its substance. If more is added, it lies without upon the surface, and forms what we call an electrical atmosphere; and then the body is said to be electrified.

8. 'Tis supposed, that all kinds of common matter do not attract and retain the electrical, with equal strength and force, for reasons to be given hereafter. And that those called electrics *per se*, as glass, &c., attract and retain it strongest, and contain the greatest quantity.

[1] See the ingenious Essays on Electricity, in the *Transactions*, by Mr. *Ellicot*.

9. We know that the electrical fluid is *in* common matter, because we can pump it *out* by the globe or tube. We know that common matter has near as much as it can contain, because, when we add a little more to any portion of it, the additional quantity does not enter, but forms an electrical atmosphere. And we know that common matter has not (generally) more than it can contain, otherwise all loose portions of it would repel each other, as they constantly do when they have electric atmospheres.

10. The beneficial uses of this electric fluid in the creation, we are not yet well acquainted with, though doubtless such there are, and those very considerable; but we may see some pernicious consequences that would attend a much greater proportion of it. For had this globe we live on, as much of it in proportion as we can give to a globe of iron, wood, or the like, the particles of dust and other light matters that get loose from it, would, by virtue of their separate electrical atmospheres, not only repel each other, but be repelled from the earth, and not easily be brought to unite with it again; whence our air would continually be more and more clogged with foreign matter, and grow unfit for respiration. This affords another occasion of adoring that wisdom which has made all things by weight and measure!

11. If a piece of common matter be supposed entirely free from electrical matter, and a single particle of the latter be brought nigh, it will be attracted, and enter the body, and take place in the center, or where the attraction is every way equal. If more particles enter, they take their places where the balance is equal between the attraction of the common matter, and their own mutual repulsion. 'Tis supposed they form triangles, whose sides shorten as their number increases; till the common matter has drawn in so many, that its whole power of compressing those triangles by attraction, is equal to their whole power of expanding themselves by repulsion; and then will such piece of matter receive no more.

12. When part of this natural proportion of electrical fluid is taken out of a piece of common matter, the triangles formed by the remainder, are supposed to widen by the mutual repulsion of the parts, until they occupy the whole piece.

13. When the quantity of electrical fluid, taken from a piece of common matter, is restored again, it enters, the expanded triangles being again compressed till there is room for the whole.

14. To explain this: take two apples, or two balls of wood or other matter, each having its own natural quantity of the electrical fluid. Suspend them by silk lines from the cieling. Apply the wire of a well-charged vial, held in your hand, to one of them (*A*) Fig. 7, and it will receive from the wire a quantity of the electrical fluid, but will not imbibe it, being already full. The fluid therefore will flow round its surface, and form an electrical atmosphere. Bring *A* into contact with *B*, and half the electrical fluid is communicated, so that each has now an electrical atmosphere, and therefore they repel each other. Take away these atmospheres by touching the balls, and leave them in their natural state: then, having fixed a stick of sealing-wax to the middle of the vial to hold it by, apply the wire to *A*, at the same time the coating touches *B*. Thus will a quantity of the electrical fluid be drawn out of *B*, and thrown on *A*. So that *A* will have a redundance of this fluid, which forms an atmosphere round it, and *B* an exactly equal deficiency. Now, bring these balls again into contact, and the electrical atmosphere will not be divided between *A* and *B*, into two smaller atmospheres as before; for *B* will drink up the whole atmosphere of *A*, and both will be found again in their natural state.

15. The form of the electrical atmosphere is that of the body it surrounds. This shape may be rendered visible in a still air, by using a smoke from dry rosin dropt into a hot tea-spoon under the electrified body, which will be attracted, and spread itself equally on all sides, covering and concealing the body. And this form it takes, because it is attracted by all parts of the surface of the body, though it cannot enter the substance already replete. Without this attraction, it would not remain round the body, but dissipate in the air.

16. The atmosphere of electrical particles surrounding an electrified sphere, is not more disposed to leave it, or more easily drawn off from any one part of the sphere than from another, because it is equally attracted by every part. But that is not the case with bodies of any other figure. From a cube it is more easily drawn at the corners

than at the plane sides and so from the angles of a body of any other form, and still most easily from the angle that is most acute. Thus, if a body shaped as A, B, C, D, E, in Fig. 8 [see p. 0], be electrified, or have an electrical atmosphere communicated to it, and we consider every side as a base on which the particles rest, and by which they are attracted, one may see, by imagining a line from A to F, and another from E to G, that the portion of the atmosphere included in F, A, E, G, has the line A E for its basis. So the portion of atmosphere included in H, A, B, I, has the line A, B, for its basis. And likewise the portion included in K, B, C, L, has B, C, to rest on; and so on the other side of the figure. Now if you would draw off this atmosphere with any blunt smooth body, and approach the middle of the side A, B, you must come very near, before the force of your attractor exceeds the force or power with which that side holds its atmosphere. But there is a small portion between I, B, K, that has less of the surface to rest on, and to be attracted by, than the neighbouring portions, while at the same time there is a mutual repulsion between its particles, and the particles of those portions; therefore here you can get it with more ease, or at a greater distance. Between F, A, H, there is a larger portion that has yet a less surface to rest on, and to attract it; here, therefore, you can get it away still more easily. But easiest of all, between L, C, M, where the quantity is largest, and the surface to attract and keep it back the least. When you have drawn away one of these angular portions of the fluid, another succeeds in its place, from the nature of fluidity, and the mutual repulsion before mentioned; and so the atmosphere continues flowing off at such angle, like a stream, till no more is remaining. The extremities of the portions of atmosphere over these angular parts, are likewise at a greater distance from the electrified body, as may be seen by the inspection of the above figure; the point of the atmosphere of the angle C being much farther from C, than any other part of the atmosphere over the lines C, B, or B, A; and, besides the distance arising from the nature of the figure, where the attraction is less, the particles will naturally expand to a greater distance by their mutual repulsion. On these accounts we suppose electrified bodies discharge their atmospheres upon unelectrified bodies more easily, and at a greater distance from their angles and points, than from their smooth sides. Those points will also discharge into the air, when the body has too great an electrical atmosphere, without bringing any non-electric near, to receive what is thrown off. For the air, though an electric *per se*, yet has always more or less water and other non-electric matters mixed with it: and these attract and receive what is so discharged.

17. But points have a property, by which they *draw on* as well as *throw off* the electrical fluid, at greater distances than blunt bodies can. That is, as the pointed part of an electrified body will discharge the atmosphere of that body, or communicate it farthest to another body, so the point of an unelectrified body will draw off the electrical atmosphere from an electrified body, farther than a blunter part of the same unelectrified body will do. Thus a pin held by the head, and the point presented to an electrified body, will draw off its atmosphere at a foot distance; where, if the head were presented instead of the point, no such effect would follow. To understand this, we may consider, that if a person standing on the floor would draw off the electrical atmosphere from an electrified body, an iron crow and a blunt knitting-needle held alternately in his hand, and presented for that purpose, do not draw with different forces in proportion to their different masses. For the man, and what he holds in his hand, be it large or small, are connected with the common mass of unelectrified matter; and the force with which he draws is the same in both cases, it consisting in the different proportion of electricity in the electrified body, and that common mass. But the force with which the electrified body retains its atmosphere by attracting it, is proportioned to the surface over which the particles are placed; that is, four square inches of that surface retain their atmosphere with four times the force that one square inch retains its atmosphere. And as in plucking the hairs from the horse's tail, a degree of strength not sufficient to pull away a handful at once, could yet easily strip it hair by hair, so a blunt body presented cannot draw off a number of particles at once, but a pointed one, with no greater force, takes them away easily, particle by particle.

18. These explanations of the power and operation of points,

when they first occurr'd to me, and while they first floated in my mind, appeared perfectly satisfactory; but now I have wrote them, and considered them more closely in black and white, I must own I have some doubts about them; yet, as I have at present nothing better to offer in their stead, I do not cross them out: for even a bad solution read, and its faults discovered, has often given rise to a good one, in the mind of an ingenious reader.

19. Nor is it of much importance to us, to know the manner in which nature executes her laws; 'tis enough if we know the laws themselves. 'Tis of real use to know that china left in the air unsupported will fall and break; but *how* it comes to fall, and *why* it breaks, are matters of speculation. 'Tis a pleasure indeed to know them, but we can preserve our china without it.

20. Thus, in the present case, to know this power of points may possibly be of some use to mankind, though we should never be able to explain it. The following experiments, as well as those in my first paper, shew this power. I have a large prime conductor, made of several thin sheets of clothier's pasteboard, form'd into a tube, near ten feet long and a foot diameter. It is cover'd with *Dutch* emboss'd paper, almost totally gilt. This large metallic surface supports a much greater electrical atmosphere than a rod of iron of 50 times the weight would do. It is suspended by silk lines, and when charged will strike at near two inches distance, a pretty hard stroke, so as to make one's knuckle ach. Let a person standing on the floor present the point of a needle, at 12 or more inches distance from it, and while the needle is so presented, the conductor cannot be charged, the point drawing off the fire as fast as it is thrown on by the electrical globe. Let it be charged, and then present the point at the same distance, and it will suddenly be discharged. In the dark you may see a light on the point, when the experiment is made. And if the person holding the point stands upon wax, he will be electrified by receiving the fire at that distance. Attempt to draw off the electricity with a blunt body, as a bolt of iron round at the end, and smooth, (a silversmith's iron punch, inch thick, is what I use) and you must bring it within the distance of three inches before you can do it, and then it is done with a stroke and

crack. As the pasteboard tube hangs loose on silk lines, when you approach it with the punch-iron, it likewise will move towards the punch, being attracted while it is charged; but if, at the same instant, a point be presented as before, it retires again, for the point discharges it. Take a pair of large brass scales, of two or more feet beam, the cords of the scales being silk. Suspend the beam by a pack-thread from the cieling, so that the bottom of the scales may be about a foot from the floor: The scales will move round in a circle by the untwisting of the pack-thread. Set the iron punch on the end upon the floor, in such a place as that the scales may pass over it in making their circle: Then electrify one scale, by applying the wire of a charged phial to it. As they move round, you see that scale draw nigher to the floor, and dip more when it comes over the punch; and if that be placed at a proper distance, the scale will snap and discharge its fire into it. But, if a needle be stuck on the end of the punch, its point upward, the scale, instead of drawing nigh to the punch, and snapping, discharges its fire silently through the point, and rises higher from the punch. Nay, even if the needle be placed upon the floor near the punch, its point upwards, the end of the punch, tho' so much higher than the needle, will not attract the scale and receive its fire, for the needle will get it and convey it away, before it comes nigh enough for the punch to act. And this is constantly observable in these experiments, that the greater quantity of electricity on the pasteboard tube, the farther it strikes or discharges its fire, and the point likewise will draw it off at a still greater distance.

Now if the fire of electricity and that of lightning be the same, as I have endeavoured to shew at large, in a former paper, this pasteboard tube and these scales may represent electrified clouds. If a tube of only ten feet long will strike and discharge its fire on the punch at two or three inches distance, an electrified cloud of perhaps 10,000 acres may strike and discharge on the earth at a proportionably greater distance. The horizontal motion of the scales over the floor, may represent the motion of the clouds over the earth; and the erect iron punch, a hill or high building; and then we see how electrified clouds passing over hills or high buildings at too great a height to strike, may be attracted lower till within their striking distance. And lastly, if a needle fixed on the punch with its point upright, or even on the floor below the punch, will draw the fire from the scale silently at a much greater than the striking distance, and so prevent its descending towards the punch; or if in its course it would have come nigh enough to strike, yet being first deprived of its fire it cannot, and the punch is thereby secured from the stroke; I say, if these things are so, may not the knowledge of this power of points be of use to mankind, in preserving houses, churches, ships, &c. from the stroke of lightning, by directing us to fix on the highest parts of those edifices, upright rods of iron made sharp as a needle, and gilt to prevent rusting, and from the foot of those rods a wire down the outside of the building into the ground, or down round one of the shrouds of a ship, and down her side till it reaches the water? Would not these pointed rods probably draw the electrical fire silently out of a cloud before it came nigh enough to strike, and thereby secure us from that most sudden and terrible mischief?

21. To determine the question, whether the clouds that contain lightning are electrified or not, I would propose an experiment to be try'd where it may be done conveniently. On the top of some high tower or steeple, place a kind of centry-box, (as in Fig. 9,) big enough to contain a man and an electrical stand. From the middle of the stand let an iron rod rise and pass bending out of the door, and then upright 20 or 30 feet, pointed very sharp at the end. If the electrical stand be kept clean and dry, a man standing on it when such clouds are passing low, might be electrified and afford sparks, the rod drawing fire to him from a cloud. If any danger to the man should be apprehended (though I think there would be none), let him stand on the floor of his box, and now and then bring near to the rod the loop of a wire that has one end fastened to the leads, he holding it by a wax handle; so the sparks, if the rod is electrified, will strike from the rod to the wire, and not affect him.

22. Before I leave this subject of lightning, I may mention some other similarities between the effects of that, and those of electricity. Lightning has often been known to strike people blind. A pigeon

that we struck dead to appearance by the electrical shock, recovering life, drooped about the yard several days, eat nothing, though crumbs were thrown to it, but declined and died. We did not think of its being deprived of sight; but afterward a pullet struck dead in like manner, being recovered by repeatedly blowing into its lungs, when set down on the floor, ran headlong against the wall, and on examination appeared perfectly blind. Hence we concluded that the pigeon also had been absolutely blinded by the shock. The biggest animal we have yet killed, or tried to kill, with the electrical stroke, was a well-grown pullet.

23. Reading in the ingenious Dr. *Miles's* account of the thunderstorm at *Stretham*, the effect of the lightning in stripping off all the paint that had covered a gilt moulding of a pannel of wainscot, without hurting the rest of the paint, I had a mind to lay a coat of paint over the filletting of gold on the cover of a book, and try the effect of a strong electrical flash sent through that gold from a charged sheet of glass. But having no paint at hand, I pasted a narrow strip of paper over it; and when dry, sent the flash through the gilding, by which the paper was torn off from end to end, with such force, that it was broke in several places, and in others brought away part of the grain of the Turky-leather in which it was bound; and convinced me, that had it been painted, the paint would have been stript off in the same manner with that on the wainscot at *Stretham*.

24. Lightning melts metals, and I hinted in my paper on that subject, that I suspected it to be a cold fusion; I do not mean a fusion by force of cold, but a fusion without heat. We have also melted gold, silver, and copper, in small quantities, by the electrical flash. The manner is this: Take leaf gold, leaf silver, or leaf gilt copper, commonly called leaf brass, or *Dutch* gold; cut off from the leaf long narrow strips, the breadth of a straw. Place one of these strips between two strips of smooth glass that are about the width of your finger. If one strip of gold, the length of the leaf, be not long enough for the glass, add another to the end of it, so that you may have a little part hanging out loose at each end of the glass. Bind the pieces of glass together from end to end with strong silk thread; then place it so as

to be part of an electrical circuit, (the ends of gold hanging out being of use to join with the other parts of the circuit,) and send the flash through it, from a large electrified jar or sheet of glass. Then if your strips of glass remain whole, you will see that the gold is missing in several places, and instead of it a metallic stain on both the glasses; the stains on the upper and under glass exactly similar in the minutest stroke, as may be seen by holding them to the light; the metal appeared to have been not only melted, but even vitrified, or otherwise so driven into the pores of the glass, as to be protected by it from the action of the strongest *Aqua Fortis* or *Aqua Regia*. I send you enclosed two little pieces of glass with these metallic stains upon them, which cannot be removed without taking part of the glass with them. Sometimes the stain spreads a little wider than the breadth of the leaf, and looks brighter at the edge, as by inspecting closely you may observe in these. Sometimes the glass breaks to pieces; once the upper glass broke into a thousand pieces, looking like coarse salt. The pieces I send you were stain'd with *Dutch* gold. True gold makes a darker stain, somewhat reddish; silver, a greenish stain. We once took two pieces of thick looking-glass, as broad as a *Gunter's* scale, and six inches long; and placing leaf gold between them, put them between two smoothly-plain'd pieces of wood, and fix'd them tight in a book-binder's small press; yet though they were so closely confined, the force of the electrical shock shivered the glass into many pieces. The gold was melted, and stain'd into the glass, as usual. The circumstances of the breaking of the glass differ much in making the experiment, and sometimes it does not break at all: but this is constant, that the stains in the upper and under pieces are exact counterparts of each other. And though I have taken up the pieces of glass between my fingers immediately after this melting, I never could perceive the least warmth in them.

25. In one of my former papers, I mentioned, that gilding on a book, though at first it communicated the shock perfectly well, yet failed after a few experiments, which we could not account for. We have since found that one strong shock breaks the continuity of the gold in the filletting, and makes it look rather like dust of gold, abun-

dance of its parts being broken and driven off; and it will seldom conduct above one strong shock. Perhaps this may be the reason: When there is not a perfect continuity in the circuit, the fire must leap over the vacancies: There is a certain distance which it is able to leap over according to its strength; if a number of small vacancies, though each be very minute, taken together exceed that distance, it cannot leap over them, and so the shock is prevented.

26. From the before-mentioned law of electricity, that points as they are more or less acute, draw on and throw off the electrical fluid with more or less power, and at greater or less distances, and in larger or smaller quantities in the same time, we may see how to account for the situation of the leaf of gold suspended between two plates, the upper one continually electrified, the under one in a person's hand standing on the floor. When the upper plate is electrified, the leaf is attracted, and raised towards it, and would fly to that plate, were it not for its own points. The corner that happens to be uppermost when the leaf is rising, being a sharp point, from the extream thinness of the gold, draws and receives at a distance a sufficient quantity of the electric fluid to give itself an electric atmosphere, by which its progress to the upper plate is stopt, and it begins to be repelled from that plate, and would be driven back to the under plate, but that its lowest corner is likewise a point, and throws off or discharges the overplus of the leaf's atmosphere, as fast as the upper corner draws it on. Were these two points perfectly equal in acuteness, the leaf would take place exactly in the middle space, for its weight is a trifle compared to the power acting on it: But it is generally nearest the unelectrified plate, because, when the leaf is offered to the electrified plate, at a distance, the sharpest point is commonly first affected and raised towards it; so *that* point, from its greater acuteness, receiving the fluid faster than its opposite can discharge it at equal distances, it retires from the electrified plate, and draws nearer to the unelectrified plate, till it comes to a distance where the discharge can be exactly equal to the receipt, the latter being lessened, and the former encreased; and there it remains as long as the globe continues to supply fresh electrical matter. This will appear

plain, when the difference of acuteness in the corners is made very great. Cut a piece of *Dutch* gold (which is fittest for these experiments on account of its greater strength) into the form of Fig. 10, the upper corner a right angle, the two next obtuse angles, and the lowest a very acute one; and bring this on your plate under the electrified plate, in such a manner as that the right-angled part may be first raised (which is done by covering the acute part with the hollow of your hand) and you will see this leaf take place much nearer to the upper than the under plate; because, without being nearer, it cannot receive so fast at its right-angled point, as it can discharge at its acute one. Turn this leaf with the acute part uppermost, and then it takes place nearest the unelectrified plate; because, otherwise, it receives faster at its acute point, than it can discharge at its right-angled one. Thus the difference of distance is always proportioned to the difference of acuteness. Take care in cutting your leaf, to leave no little ragged particles on the edges, which sometimes form points where you would not have them. You may make this figure so acute below, and blunt above, as to need no under plate, it discharging fast enough into the air. When it is made narrower, as the figure between the pricked lines, we call it the *Golden Fish*, from its manner of acting. For if you take it by the tail, and hold it at a foot or greater horizontal distance from the prime conductor, it will, when let go, fly to it with a brisk but wavering motion, like that of an eel through the water; it will then take place under the prime conductor, at perhaps a quarter or half of an inch distance, and keep a continual shaking of its tail like a fish, so that it seems animated. Turn its tail towards the prime conductor, and then it flies to your finger, and seems to nibble it. And if you hold a plate under it at six or eight inches distance, and cease turning the globe, when the electrical atmosphere of the conductor grows small, it will descend to the plate, and swim back again several times, with the same fish-like motion, greatly to the entertainment of spectators. By a little practice in blunting or sharpening the heads or tails of these figures, you may make them take place as desired, nearer or farther from the electrified plate.

27. It is said, in Section 8 of this paper, that all kinds of common

matter are supposed not to attract the electrical fluid with equal strength; and that those called electrics *per se*, as glass, &c., attract and retain it strongest, and contain the greatest quantity. This latter position may seem a paradox to some, being contrary to the hitherto received opinion; and therefore I shall now endeavour to explain it.

28. In order to this, let it first be consider'd, *that we cannot, by any means we are yet acquainted with, force the electrical fluid thro' glass.* I know it is commonly thought, that it easily pervades glass; and the experiment of a feather suspended by a thread, in a bottle hermetically sealed, yet moved by bringing a rubbed tube near the outside of the bottle, is alledged to prove it. But, if the electrical fluid so easily pervades glass, how does the vial become *charged* (as we term it), when we hold it in our hands? Would not the fire thrown in by the wire, pass through to our hands, and so escape into the floor? Would not the bottle in that case be left just as we found it, uncharged, as we know a metal bottle so attempted to be charged would be? Indeed, if there be the least crack, the minutest solution of continuity in the glass, though it remains so tight that nothing else we know of will pass, yet the extremely subtile electric fluid flies through such a crack with the greatest freedom, and such a bottle we know can never be charged: What then makes the difference between such a bottle and one that is sound, but this, that the fluid can pass through the one, and not through the other?

29. It is true, there is an experiment, that at first sight would be apt to satisfy a slight observer, that the fire thrown into the bottle by the wire, does really pass thro' the glass. It is this: place the bottle on a glass stand, under the prime conductor; suspend a bullet by a chain from the prime conductor, till it comes within a quarter of an inch right over the wire of the bottle; place your knuckle on the glass stand, at just the same distance from the coating of the bottle, as the bullet is from its wire. Now let the globe be turned, and you see a spark strike from the bullet to the wire of the bottle, and the same instant you see and feel an exactly equal spark striking from the coating on your knuckle, and so on, spark for spark. This looks as if the whole received by the bottle was again discharged from it.

And yet the bottle by this means is charged! And therefore the fire that thus leaves the bottle, though the same in quantity, cannot be the very same fire that entered at the wire, for if it were, the bottle would remain uncharged.

30. If the fire that so leaves the bottle be not the same that is thrown in through the wire, it must be fire that subsisted in the bottle (that is, in the glass of the bottle) before the operation began.

31. If so, there must be a great quantity in glass, because a great quantity is thus discharged, even from very thin glass.

32. That this electrical fluid or fire is strongly attracted by glass, we know from the quickness and violence with which it is resumed by the part that had been deprived of it, when there is an opportunity. And by this, that we cannot from a mass of glass, draw a quantity of electric fire, or electrify the whole mass *minus*, as we can a mass of metal. We cannot lessen or increase its whole quantity, for the quantity it has it holds; and it has as much as it can hold. Its pores are filled with it as full as the mutual repellency of the particles will admit; and what is already in, refuses, or strongly repels, any additional quantity. Nor have we any way of moving the electrical fluid in glass, but one; that is, by covering part of the two surfaces of thin glass with non-electrics, and then throwing an additional quantity of this fluid on one surface, which spreading in the non-electric, and being bound by it to that surface, acts by its repelling force on the particles of the electrical fluid contained in the other surface, and drives them out of the glass into the non-electric on that side, from whence they are discharged, and then those added on the charged side can enter. But when this is done, there is no more in the glass, nor less than before, just as much having left it on one side as it received on the other.

33. I feel a want of terms here, and doubt much whether I shall be able to make this part intelligible. By the word *surface*, in this case, I do not mean mere length and breadth without thickness; but when I speak of the upper or under surface of a piece of glass, the outer or inner surface of the vial, I mean length, breadth, and half the thickness, and beg the favour of being so understood. Now, I suppose, that

glass in its first principles, and in the furnace, has no more of this electrical fluid than other common matter: That when it is blown, as it cools, and the particles of common fire leave it, its pores become a vacuum: That the component parts of glass are extremely small, and fine, I guess from its never showing a rough face when it breaks, but always a polish; and from the smallness of its particles I suppose the pores between them must be exceeding small, which is the reason that aqua-fortis, nor any other menstruum we have, can enter to separate them and dissolve the substance; nor is any fluid we know of, fine enough to enter, except common fire, and the electric fluid. Now the departing fire, leaving a vacuum, as aforesaid, between these pores, which air nor water are fine enough to enter and fill, the electric fluid, (which is everywhere ready in what we call the non-electrics, and in the non-electric mixtures that are in the air) is attracted in; yet does not become fixed with the substance of the glass, but subsists there as water in a porous stone, retained only by the attraction of the fixed parts, itself still loose and a fluid. But I suppose farther, that in the cooling of the glass, its texture becomes closest in the middle, and forms a kind of partition, in which the pores are so narrow, that the particles of the electrical fluid, which enter both surfaces at the same time, cannot go through, or pass and repass from one surface to the other, and so mix together; yet, though the particles of electric fluid, imbibed by each surface, cannot themselves pass through to those of the other, their repellency can, and by this means they act on one another. The particles of the electic fluid have a mutual repellency, but by the power of attraction in the glass they are condensed or forced nearer to each other. When the glass has received, and, by its attraction, forced closer together so much of this electric fluid, as that the power of attracting and condensing in the one, is equal to the power of expansion in the other, it can imbibe no more, and that remains its constant whole quantity; but each surface would receive more, if the repellency of what is in the opposite surface did not resist its entrance. The quantities of this fluid in each surface being equal, their repelling action on each other is equal; and therefore those of one surface cannot drive out those of the other; but, if a greater quantity is forced into one surface than the glass would naturally draw in, this increases the repelling power on that side, and, overpowering the attraction on the other, drives out part of the fluid that had been imbibed by that surface, if there be any non-electric ready to receive it; such there is in all cases where glass is electrified to give a shock. The surface that has been thus emptied by having its electrical fluid driven out, resumes again an equal quantity with violence, as soon as the glass has an opportunity to discharge that over quantity more than it could retain by attraction in its other surface, by the additional repellency of which the vacuum had been occasioned. For experiments favouring (if I may not say confirming) this hypothesis, I must, to avoid repetition, beg leave to refer you back to what is said of the electrical phial in my former papers.

34. Let us now see how it will account for several other appearances. Glass, a body extremely elastic (and perhaps its elasticity may be owing in some degree to the subsisting of so great a quantity of this repelling fluid in its pores) must, when rubbed, have its rubbed surface somewhat stretched, or its solid parts drawn a little farther asunder, so that the vacancies, in which the electrical fluid resides, become larger, affording room for more of that fluid, which is immediately attracted into it from the cushion or hand rubbing, they being supplied from the common stock. But the instant the parts of the glass so opened and filled, have passed the friction, they close again, and force the additional quantity out upon the surface, where it must rest till that part comes round to the cushion again, unless some non-electric (as the prime conductor) first presents to receive it.[1] But if the inside of the globe be lined with a non-electric, the additional repellency of the electrical fluid, thus collected by friction on the

---

[1] In the dark, the electric fluid may be seen on the cushion in two semicircles or half-moons, one on the fore part, the other on the back part of the cushion, just where the globe and cushion separate. In the fore crescent the fire is passing out of the cushion into the glass; in the other it is leaving the glass, and returning into the back part of the cushion. When the prime conductor is apply'd to take it off the glass, the back crescent disappears.

rubb'd part of the globe's outer surface, drives an equal quantity out of the inner surface into that non-electric lining, which receiving it, and carrying it away from the rubb'd part into the common mass, through the axis of the globe, and frame of the machine, the new-collected electrical fluid can enter and remain in the outer surface, and none of it (or a very little) will be received by the prime conductor. As this charg'd part of the globe comes round to the cushion again, the outer surface delivers its overplus fire into the cushion, the opposite inner surface receiving at the same time an equal quantity from the floor. Every electrician knows, that a globe wet within will afford little or no fire; but the reason has not before been attempted to be given, that I know of.

34 (sic). So if a tube lined with a non-electric be rubb'd,[1] little or no fire is obtained from it. What is collected from the hand, in the downward rubbing stroke, entering the pores of the glass, and driving an equal quantity out of the inner surface into the non-electric lining: and the hand in passing up to take a second stroke, takes out again what had been thrown into the outer surface, and then the inner surface receives back again what it had given to the non-electric lining. Thus the particles of electrical fluid belonging to the inside surface go in and out of their pores every stroke given to the tube. Put a wire into the tube, the inward end in contact with the non-electric lining, so it will represent the *Leyden* bottle. Let a second person touch the wire while you rub, and the fire driven out of the inward surface when you give the stroke, will pass through him into the common mass, and return through him when the inner surface resumes its quantity, and therefore this new kind of *Leyden* bottle cannot be so charged. But thus it may: after every stroke, before you pass your hand up to make another, let a second person apply his finger to the wire, take the spark, and then withdraw his finger; and so on till he has drawn a number of sparks; thus will the inner surface be exhausted, and the outer surface charged; then wrap a sheet of gilt paper close round the outer surface, and grasping it in your hand you may

[1] Gilt Paper, with the gilt face next the glass, does well.

receive a shock by applying the finger of the other hand to the wire: for now the vacant pores in the inner surface resume their quantity, and the overcharg'd pores in the outer surface discharge that overplus; the equilibrium being restored through your body, which could not be restored through the glass. If the tube be exhausted of air, a non-electric lining, in contact with the wire, is not necessary; for *in vacuo*, the electrical fire will fly freely from the inner surface, without a non-electric conductor: but air resists in motion; for being itself an electric *per se*, it does not attract it, having already its quantity. So the air never draws off an electric atmosphere from any body, but in proportion to the non-electrics mix'd with it: it rather keeps such an atmosphere confin'd, which from the mutual repulsion of its particles, tends to dissipation, and would immediately dissipate *in vacuo*. And thus the experiment of the feather inclosed in a glass vessel hermetically sealed, but moving on the approach of the rubbed tube, is explained: When an additional quantity of the electrical fluid is applied to the side of the vessel by the atmosphere of the tube, a quantity is repelled and driven out of the inner surface of that side into the vessel, and there affects the feather, returning again into its pores, when the tube with its atmosphere is withdrawn; not that the particles of that atmosphere did themselves pass through the glass to the feather. And every other appearance I have yet seen, in which glass and electricity are concerned, are, I think, explained with equal ease by the same hypothesis. Yet, perhaps, it may not be a true one, and I shall be obliged to him that affords me a better.

35. Thus I take the difference between non-electrics, and glass, an electric *per se*, to consist in these two particulars. 1st, That a non-electric easily suffers a change in the quantity of the electric fluid it contains. You may lessen its whole quantity, by drawing out a part, which the whole body will again resume; but of glass you can only lessen the quantity contained in one of its surfaces; and not that, but by supplying an equal quantity at the same time to the other surface; so that the whole glass may always have the same quantity in the two surfaces, their two different quantities being added together. And this can only be done in glass that is thin; beyond a certain

thickness we have yet no power that can make this change. And, 2dly, that the electric fire freely removes from place to place, in and through the substance of a non-electric, but not so through the substance of glass. If you offer a quantity to one end of a long rod of metal, it receives it, and when it enters, every particle that was before in the rod, pushes its neighbour quite to the farther end, where the overplus is discharged; and this instantaneously where the rod is part of the circle in the experiment of the shock. But glass, from the smallness of its pores, or stronger attraction of what it contains, refuses to admit so free a motion; a glass rod will not conduct a shock, nor will the thinnest glass suffer any particle entering one of its surfaces to pass through to the other.

36. Hence we see the impossibility of success in the experiments proposed, to draw out the effluvial virtues of a non-electric, as cinnamon for instance, and mixing them with the electric fluid, to convey them with that into the body, by including it in the globe, and then applying friction, &c. For though the effluvia of cinnamon, and the electric fluid should mix within the globe, they would never come out together through the pores of the glass, and so go to the prime conductor; for the electric fluid itself cannot come through; and the prime conductor is always supply'd from the cushion, and that from the floor. And besides, when the globe is filled with cinnamon, or other non-electric, no electric fluid can be obtained from its outer surface, for the reason before mentioned. I have tried another way, which I thought more likely to obtain a mixture of the electric and other effluvia together, if such a mixture had been possible. I placed a glass plate under my cushion, to cut off the communication between the cushion and floor; then brought a small chain from the cushion into a glass of oil of turpentine, and carried another chain from the oil of turpentine to the floor, taking care that the chain from the cushion to the glass touch'd no part of the frame of the machine. Another chain was fixed to the prime conductor, and held in the hand of a person to be electrified. The ends of the two chains in the glass were near an inch distant from each other, the oil of turpentine between. Now the globe being turned, could draw no fire from the floor through

the machine, the communication that way being cut off by the thick glass plate under the cushion: it must then draw it through the chains whose ends were dipped in the oil of turpentine. And as the oil of turpentine, being an electric *per se*, would not conduct, what came up from the floor was obliged to jump from the end of one chain to the end of the other, through the substance of that oil, which we could see in large sparks, and so it had a fair opportunity of seizing some of the finest particles of the oil in its passage, and carrying them off with it: but no such effect followed, nor could I perceive the least difference in the smell of the electric effluvia thus collected, from what it has when collected otherwise, nor does it otherwise affect the body of a person electrised. I likewise put into a phial, instead of water, a strong purgative liquid, and then charged the phial, and took repeated shocks from it, in which case every particle of the electrical fluid must, before it went through my body, have first gone through the liquid when the phial is charging, and returned through it when discharging, yet no other effect followed than if it had been charged with water. I have also smelt the electric fire when drawn thro' gold, silver, copper, lead, iron, wood, and the human body, and could perceive no difference; the odour is always the same where the spark does not burn what it strikes; and therefore I imagine it does not take that smell from any quality of the bodies it passes through. And indeed, as that smell so readily leaves the electric matter, and adheres to the knuckle receiving the sparks, and to other things; I suspect that it never was connected with it, but arises instantaneously from something in the air acted upon by it. For if it was fine enough to come with the electric fluid through the body of one person, why should it stop on the skin of another?

But I shall never have done, if I tell you all my conjectures, thoughts, and imaginations on the nature and operations of this electric fluid, and relate the variety of little experiments we have tried. I have already made this paper too long, for which I must crave pardon, not having now time to make it shorter. I shall only add, that as it has been observed here that spirits will fire by the electric spark in the summertime, without heating them, when *Fahrenheit's* thermometer is above 70; so when colder, if the operator puts a small flat bottle of spirits in his bosom, or a close pocket, with the spoon, some little time before he uses them, the heat of his body will communicate warmth more than sufficient for the purpose.

ADDITIONAL EXPERIMENTS

Proving that the Leyden Bottle has no more Electrical Fire in it when charged, than before; nor less when discharged: That, in discharging, the Fire does not issue from the Wire and the Coating at the same Time, as some have thought, but that the Coating always receives what is discharged by the Wire, or an equal Quantity; the outer Surface being always in a Negative State of Electricity, when the inner Surface is in a Positive State.

PLACE a thick plate of glass under the rubbing cushion, to cut off the communication of electrical fire from the floor to the cushion; then, if there be no fine points or hairy threads sticking out from the cushion, or from the parts of the machine opposite to the cushion, (of which you must be careful) you can get but a few sparks from the prime conductor, which are all the cushion will part with.

Hang a phial then on the prime conductor, and it will not charge though you hold it by the coating. But

Form a communication by a chain from the coating to the cushion, and the phial will charge.

For the globe then draws the electric fire out of the outside surface of the phial, and forces it through the prime conductor and wire of the phial, into the inside surface.

Thus the bottle is charged with its own fire, no other being to be had while the glass plate is under the cushion.

Hang two cork balls by flaxen threads to the prime conductor; then touch the coating of the bottle, and they will be electrified and recede from each other.

For, just as much fire as you give the coating, so much is discharged through the wire upon the prime conductor, whence the cork balls receive an electrical atmosphere. But,

Take a wire bent in the form of a C, with a stick of wax fixed to the outside of the curve, to hold it by; and apply one end of this wire to the coating, and the other at the same time to the prime conductor, the phial will be discharged; and if the balls are not electrified before the discharge, neither will they appear to be so after the discharge, for they will not repel each other.

Now if the fire discharged from the inside surface of the bottle through its wire, remained on the prime conductor, the balls would be electrified, and recede from each other.

If the phial really exploded at both ends, and discharged fire from both coating and wire, the balls would be *more* electrified, and recede *farther;* for none of the fire can escape, the wax handle preventing.

But if the fire, with which the inside surface is surcharged, be so much precisely as is wanted by the outside surface, it will pass round through the wire fixed to the wax handle, restore the equilibrium in the glass, and make no alteration in the state of the prime conductor.

Accordingly we find, that, if the prime conductor be electrified, and the cork balls in a state of repellency before the bottle is discharged, they continue so afterwards. If not, they are not electrified by that discharge.

To PETER COLLINSON. *October 19, 1752*

As frequent mention is made in public papers from *Europe* of the success of the *Philadelphia* experiment for drawing the electric fire from clouds by means of pointed rods of iron erected on high buildings &c., it may be agreeable to the curious to be informed, that the same experiment has succeeded in *Philadelphia*, though made in a different and more easy manner, which is as follows:

Make a small cross of two light strips of cedar, the arms so long as to reach to the four corners of a large thin silk handkerchief when extended; tie the corners of the handkerchief to the extremities of the cross, so you have the body of a kite; which being properly accommodated with a tail, loop, and string, will rise in the air, like those made of paper; but this being of silk, is fitter to bear the wet and wind of a thunder-gust without tearing. To the top of the upright stick of the cross is to be fixed a very sharp-pointed wire, rising a foot or more above the wood. To the end of the twine, next the hand, is to be tied a silk ribbon, and where the silk and twine join, a key may be fastened. This kite is to be raised when a thunder-gust appears to be coming on, and the person who holds the string must stand within a door or window, or under some cover, so that the silk ribbon may not be wet; and care must be taken that the twine does not touch the frame of the door or window. As soon as any of the thunder-clouds come over the kite, the pointed wire will draw the electric fire from them, and the kite, with all the twine, will be electrified, and the loose filaments of the twine will stand out every way, and be attracted by an approaching finger. And when the rain has wet the kite and twine, so that it can conduct the electric fire freely, you will find it stream out plentifully from the key on the approach of your knuckle. At this key the phial may be charged; and from electric fire thus obtained, spirits may be kindled, and all the other electric experiments be performed, which are usually done by the help of a rubbed glass globe or tube, and thereby the sameness of the electric matter with that of lightning completely demonstrated.

FRANKLIN. *Pennsylvania Gazette, October 19, 1752*

THE Doctor, after having published his method of verifying his hypothesis concerning the sameness of electricity with the matter of lightning, was waiting for the erection of a spire in Philadelphia to carry his views into execution; not imagining that a pointed rod, of a moderate height, could answer the purpose; when it occurred to him, that, by means of a common kite, he could have a readier and better access to the regions of thunder than by any spire whatever.

Preparing, therefore, a large silk handkerchief, and two cross sticks, of a proper length, on which to extended it; he took the opportunity of the first approaching thunder storm to take a walk into a field, in which there was a shed convenient for his purpose. But dreading the ridicule which too commonly attends unsuccessful attempts in science, he communicated his intended experiment to no body but his son, who assisted him in raising the kite.

The kite being raised, a considerable time elapsed before there was any appearance of its being electrified. One very promising cloud had passed over it without any effect; when, at length, just as he was beginning to despair of his contrivance, he observed some lose threads of the hempen string to stand erect, and to avoid one another, just as if they had been suspended on a common conductor. Struck with this promising appearance, he immediately presented his knucle to the key, and (let the reader judge of the exquisite pleasure he must have felt at that moment) the discovery was complete. He perceived a very evident electric spark. Others succeeded, even before the string was wet, so as to put the matter past all dispute, and when the rain had wet the string, he collected electric fire very copiously. This happened in June 1752, a month after the electricians in France had verified the same theory, but before he heard of any thing they had done.

Besides this kite, Dr. Franklin had afterwards an insulated iron rod to draw the lightning into his house, in order to make experiments whenever there should be a considerable quantity of it in the atmosphere; and that he might not lose any opportunity of that nature, he connected two bells with this apparatus, which gave him notice, by their ringing, whenever his rod was electrified.[1]

[1] Franklin's Letters, p. 112.

CHAPTER 8

Air Ways

(a) Whirlwind

During a clear, summer afternoon, when the ground has been greatly heated, a dust whirl may develop and travel some distance until it is no longer distinguishable. The low-lying hot air is less dense than that above it. The atmosphere, therefore, is vertically unstable, giving rise to convection. Incoming air is likely to be directed to one side of the center, thus establishing angular momentum, which ideally would remain the same if not disturbed. The air, gathering up dust, leaves, and other light materials, continues to rotate more or less constantly, clockwise or counter-clockwise as the case may be. A tornado is the most violent, least extensive, and most sharply defined of all storms. Its circular column of upward spiraling winds has destructive speeds. Over water it is called a waterspout. Franklin held the popular notion that the latter contained water. It is, however, only a cloud of water drops and droplets.

To PETER COLLINSON. *25 August, 1755*

As you have my former papers on Whirlwinds, &c., I now send you an account of one which I had lately an opportunity of seeing and examining myself.

Being in *Maryland*, riding with Colonel *Tasker*, and some other gentlemen to his country-seat, where I and my son were entertained by that amiable and worthy man with great hospitality and kindness, we saw in the vale below us, a small whirlwind beginning in the road, and shewing itself by the dust it raised and contained. It appeared in the form of a sugar-loaf, spinning on its point, moving up the hill towards us, and enlarging as it came forward. When it passed by us, its smaller part near the ground, appeared no bigger than a common barrel, but widening upwards, it seemed, at 40 or 50 feet high, to be 20 or 30 feet in diameter. The rest of the company stood looking after it, but my curiosity being stronger, I followed it, riding close by its side, and observed its licking up, in its progress, all the dust that was under its smaller part. As it is a common opinion that a shot, fired through a water-spout, will break it, I tried to break this little whirlwind, by striking my whip frequently through it, but without any effect. Soon after, it quitted the road and took into the woods, growing every moment larger and stronger, raising, instead of dust, the old dry leaves with which the ground was thick covered, and making a great noise with them and the branches of the trees, bending some tall trees round in a circle swiftly and very surprizingly, though the progressive motion of the whirl was not so swift but that a man on foot might have kept pace with it; but the circular motion was amazingly rapid. By the leaves it was now filled with, I could plainly perceive that the current of air they were driven by, moved upwards in a spiral line; and when I saw the trunks and bodies of large trees invelop'd in the passing whirl, which continued intire after it had left them I no longer wondered that my whip had no effect on it in its smaller state. I accompanied it about three quarters of a mile, till some limbs of dead trees, broken off by the whirl, flying about and falling near me, made me more apprehensive of danger; and then I stopped, looking at the top of it as it went on, which was visible, by means of the leaves contained in it, for a very great height above the trees. Many of the leaves, as they got loose from the upper and widest part, were scattered in the wind; but so great was their height in the air, that they appeared no bigger than flies. My son, who was by this time come up with me, followed the whirlwind till it left the woods, and crossed an old tobacco-field, where, finding neither dust nor leaves to take up, it gradually became invisible below as it went away over that field. The course of the general wind then blowing was along with us as we travelled, and the progressive motion of the whirlwind was in a direction nearly opposite, though it did not keep a strait line, nor was its progressive motion uniform, it making little sallies on either hand as it went, proceeding sometimes faster and sometimes slower, and seeming sometimes for a few seconds almost stationary, then starting forward pretty fast again. When we rejoined the company, they were admiring the vast height of the leaves now brought by the common wind, over our heads. These leaves accompanied us as we travelled, some falling now and then round about us, and some not reaching the ground till we had gone near three miles from the place where we first saw the whirlwind begin. Upon my asking Colonel *Tasker* if such whirlwinds were common in *Maryland*, he answered pleasantly, "No, not at all common; but we got this on purpose to treat Mr. Franklin." And a very high treat it was.

(b) Wind and Storm

In 1743 Franklin was surprised to find a wind from the northeast associated with a storm that was actually from the southwest—the beginning of our understanding of atmospheric circulation.

It is common knowledge today that a cyclone in the northern hemisphere consists of a vast counter-clockwise whirl of rapidly moving air currents about a relatively small center of low pressure. Those originating in the Gulf of Mexico move more or less toward the northeast. In such a case, however, the wind at a particular place may be blowing from any direction, say from the northeast, or from the southwest.

To JARED ELIOT. *February 13, 1749/50*

You desire to know my Thoughts about the N.E. Storms beginning to Leeward. Some Years since there was an Eclipse of the Moon at 9 in the Evining, which I intended to observe, but before 8 a Storm blew up at N E. and continued violent all Night and all next Day, the Sky thick clouded, dark and rainy, so that neither Moon nor Stars could be seen. The Storm did a great deal of Damage all along the Coast, for we had Accounts of it in the News Papers from Boston, Newport, New York, Maryland and Virginia. But what surpriz'd me, was to find in the Boston Newspapers an Account of an Observation of that Eclipse made there: For I thought, as the Storm came from the N E. it must have begun sooner at Boston than with us, and consequently have prevented such Observation. I wrote to my Brother about it, and he inform'd me, that the Eclipse was over there, an hour before the Storm began. Since which I have made Enquiries from time to time of Travellers, and of my Correspondents N Eastward and S. Westward, and observ'd the Accounts in the Newspapers from N England, N York, Maryland, Virginia and South Carolina, and I find it to be a constant Fact, that N East Storms begin to Leeward; and are often more violent there than farther to Windward. Thus the last October Storm, which with you was on the 8th. began on the 7th in Virginia and N Carolina, and was most violent there. As to the Reason of this, I can only give you my Conjectures. Suppose a great Tract of Country, Land and Sea, to wit Florida and the Bay of Mexico, to have clear Weather for several Days, and to be heated by the Sun and its Air thereby exceedingly rarified; Suppose the Country North Eastward, as Pensilvania, New England, Nova Scotia, Newfoundland, &c. to be at the same time cover'd with Clouds, and its Air chill'd and condens'd. The rarified Air being lighter must rise, and the Dense Air next to it will press into its Place; that will be follow'd by the next denser Air, that by the next, and so on. Thus when I have a Fire in my Chimney, there is a Current of Air constantly flowing from the Door to the Chimney: but the beginning of the Motion was at the Chimney, where the Air being rarified by the Fire, rising, its Place was supply'd by the cooler Air that was next to it, and the Place of that by the next, and so on to the Door. So the Water in a long Sluice or Mill Race, being stop'd by a Gate, is at Rest like the Air in a Calm; but as soon as you open the Gate at one End to let it out, the Water next the Gate begins first to move, that which

is next to it follows; and so tho' the Water proceeds forward to the
Gate, the Motion which began there runs backwards, if one may so
speak, to the upper End of the Race, where the Water is last in Motion.
We have on this Continent a long Ridge of Mountains running from
N East to S. West; and the Coast runs the same Course. These may,
perhaps, contribute towards the Direction [of the winds or at least
influence] them in some Degree, [missing]. If these Conjectures do
not [satisfy you, I wish] to have yours on the Subject.

(c) Fog and Smoke

Franklin accounted for the coolness of the summer of 1783 by a
constant fog over all Europe, which he ascribed possibly to volcanic
smoke.

METEOROLOGICAL IMAGINATION AND CONJECTURES. *May 1784*

There seems to be a Region high in the Air over all Countries,
where it is always Winter, where Frost exists continually, since in the
midst of Summer, on the Surface of the Earth, Ice falls often from
above, in the Form of Hail.

Hailstones, of the great Weight we sometimes find them, did not
probably acquire their Magnitude before they began to descend. The
Air, 800 times rarer than Water, is unable to support it but in the
Shape of Vapour, a State in which its Particles are separated. As soon
as they are condensed by the Cold of the upper Regions, so as to
form a Drop, that Drop begins to fall. If it freezes into a Grain of
Ice, that Ice descends. In descending, both the Drop of Water and the
Grain of Ice are augmented by Particles of the Vapour they pass thro'
in falling, and which they condense by their Coldness, and attach to
themselves.

It is possible that, in Summer, much of what is Rain when it arrives at the Surface of the Earth, might have been Snow when it began
its Descent; but, being thaw'd in passing thro' the warm Air near
the Surface, it is changed from Snow into Rain.

How immensely cold must be the original Particle of Hail, which forms the Centre of the future Hailstone, since it is capable of communicating sufficient Cold, if I may so speak, because perhaps it is not by communicating Cold to the Particles of Vapour that it freezes them but by depriving them of their Heat, to freeze all the Mass of Vapour condensed round it, and form a Lump of perhaps 6 or 8 ounces in weight!

When, in Summer time, the Son is high, and long every Day above the Horizon, his Rays strike the Earth more directly, and with longer Continuance, than in Winter; hence the Surface is more heated, and to a greater Depth, by the effect of those Rays.

When Rain falls on the heated Earth, and soaks down into it, if carries down with it a great part of the Heat, which by that means descends still deeper.

The Mass of Earth, to the depth perhaps of 30 Feet, being thus heated to a certain Degree, continues to retain its Heat for some time. Thus the first Snows, that fall in the Beginning of Winter, seldom lie long on the Surface, but are soon melted, and soon absorbed. After which, the Winds, that blow over the Country on which the Snows had fallen, are not rend'red so cold as they would have been, by those Snows, if they had remained. The Earth, too, thus uncovered by the Snows, which would have reflected the Sun's Rays, now absorbs them, receiving and retaining the Warmth they afford and thus the Approach of the Severity of Winter is retarded; and the extreme degree of its Cold is not always at the time we might expect it, viz. when the Sun is at its greatest Distance, and the Days shortest, but some time after that Period, according to the English Proverb, which says, "As the Day lengthens, the Cold strengthens;" the Causes of refrigeration continuing to operate, while the Sun returns too slowly, and his Force continues too weak, to counteract them.

During several of the Summer Months of the Year 1783, when the Effect of the Sun's Rays to heat the Earth in these northern Regions should have been greatest, there existed a constant Fog over all Europe. This Fog was of a permanent Nature; it was dry, and the Rays of the Sun seem'd to have little Effect towards dissipating it, as they easily do a moist Fog, arising from Water. They were indeed rend'red so faint in passing thro' it, that, when collected in the Focus of a Burning-Glass, they would scarce kindle brown Paper. Of course, their Summer Effect in heating the Earth was exceedingly diminished.

Hence the Surface was early frozen.

Hence the first Snows remained on it unmelted, and received continual Additions.

Hence the Air was more chilled and the Winds more severely cold. Hence perhaps the Winter of 1783-4, was more severe than any that had happened for many years.

The Cause of this Universal Fog is not yet ascertained. Whether it was adventitious to this Earth, and merely a Smoke proceeding from the Consumption by Fire of some of those great burning Balls or Globes which we happen to meet with in our rapid Course round the Sun, and which are sometimes seen to kindle and be destroy'd in passing our Atmosphere, and whose Smoke might be attracted and retain'd by our Earth: or whether it was the vast Quantity of Smoke, long continuing to issue during the Summer from Hecla, in Iceland, and that other Volcano which arose out of the Sea near that Island, which Smoke might be spread by various Winds, over the northern Part of the World, is yet uncertain.

It seems however worth the Enquiry, whether other hard Winters, recorded in History, were preceded by similar permanent and widely extended Summer Fogs. Because, if found to be so, Men might from such Fogs conjecture the Probability of a succeeding hard Winter, and of the damages to be expected by the breaking up of frozen Rivers at the Approach of Spring; and take such Measures as are possible and practicable, to secure themselves and Effects from the Mischiefs that attended the last.

(d) Flashes and Bells

In September 1752 Franklin had a lightning rod attached to his house on Market Street; bells were made to ring when the rod became electrified. A Leyden jar could be simultaneously charged, and the kind of electrification of the cloud thereby determined. This work was the only direct and reliable information on atmospheric electricity for a period of 170 years. The physician to Louis XV, Louis Guillaume le Monnier (1717–99), who had successfully repeated Dalibard's experiment, observed also that atmospheric electricity may exist even without a cloud.

In a letter on thunder gusts, Franklin told of an experiment he had performed with a model of a cloud. Unfortunately, the model was based on a surface distribution of charge and is not quite comparable with a real cloud, which has its charge distributed throughout its entire volume.

Sir Charles Vernon Boys (1855–1944) later used a camera (1902) to investigate the phenomenon of lightning. The electric field about the earth has been determined by having pointed rods attached to recording galvanometers. The quantity of electricity moving to and from the earth has been actually measured by means of a water voltameter. The kind and amount of electric charge in the very heart of a cloud has been determined by the use of points on balloons. Paradoxically, we are now investigating lightning phenomena more to determine the nature of electricity than vice versa.

To JOHN MITCHELL. *April 29, 1749*

32. If a country be plain, having no mountains to intercept the electrified clouds, yet it is not without means to make them deposite their water. For if an electrified cloud coming from the sea, meets in the air a cloud raised from the land, and therefore not electrified; the first will flash its fire into the latter, and thereby both clouds shall be made suddenly to deposite water.

33. The electrified particles of the first cloud close when they lose their fire; the particles of the other clouds close in receiving it: in both, they have thereby an opportunity of coalescing into drops. The concussion or jerk given to the air, contributes also to shake down the water, not only from those two clouds, but from others near them. Hence the sudden fall of rain immediately after flashes of lightning.

34. To shew this by an easy experiment: Take two round pieces

of pasteboard, two inches diameter; from the center and circumference of each of them suspend by fine silk threads eighteen inches long, seven small balls of wood, or seven peas equal in bigness: so will the balls, appending to each pasteboard, form equal equilateral triangles, one ball being in the center, and six at equal distances from that, and from each other; and thus they represent particles of air. Dip both sets in water, and some adhering to each ball, they will represent air loaded. Dexterously electrify one set, and its balls will repel each other to a greater distance, enlarging the triangles. Could the water supported by seven balls come into contact, it would form a drop or drops so heavy as to break the cohesion it had with the balls, and so fall. Let the two sets then represent two clouds, the one a sea cloud electrified, the other a land cloud. Bring them within the sphere of attraction, and they will draw towards each other, and you will see the separated balls close thus; the first electrified ball that comes near an unelectrified ball by attraction joins it, and gives it fire; instantly they separate, and each flies to another ball of its own party, one to give, the other to receive fire; and so it proceeds through both sets, but so quick as to be in a manner instantaneous. In the cohesion they shake off and drop their water, which represents rain.

35. Thus, when sea and land clouds would pass at too great a distance from the flash, they are attracted towards each other till within that distance; for the sphere of electrical attraction is far beyond the distance of flashing.

36. When a great number of clouds from the sea meet a number of clouds raised from the land, the electrical flashes appear to strike in different parts; and as the clouds are jostled and mixed by the winds, or brought near by the electrical attraction, they continue to give and receive flash after flash, till the electrical fire is equally diffused.

37. When the gun-barrel (in electrical experiments) has but little electrical fire in it, you must approach it very near with your knuckle, before you can draw a spark. Give it more fire, and it will give a spark at a greater distance. Two gun-barrels united, and as highly electrified, will give a spark at a still greater distance. But, if two gun-barrels electrified will strike at two inches distance, and make a loud

snap, to what a great distance may 10,000 acres of electrified cloud strike and give its fire, and how loud must be that crack?

38. It is a common thing to see clouds at different heights passing different ways, which shews different currents of air, one under the other. As the air between the tropics is rarified by the sun, it rises, the denser northern and southern air pressing into its place. The air, so rarified and forced up, passes northward and southward, and must descend into the polar regions, if it has no opportunity before, that the circulation may be carried on.

39. As currents of air, with the clouds therein, pass different ways, 'tis easy to conceive how the clouds, passing over each other, may attract each other, and so come near enough for the electrical stroke. And also how electrical clouds may be carried within land very far from the sea, before they have an opporunity to strike.

40. When the air, with its vapours raised from the ocean between the tropics, comes to descend in the polar regions, and to be in contact with the vapours arising there, the electrical fire they brought begins to be communicated, and is seen in clear nights, being first visible where 'tis first in motion, that is, where the contact begins, or in the most northern part; from thence the streams of light seem to shoot southerly, even up to the zenith of northern countries. But tho' the light seems to shoot from the north southerly, the progress of the fire is really from the south northerly, its motion beginning in the north being the reason that 'tis there first seen.

For the electrical fire is never visible but when in motion, and leaping from body to body, or from particle to particle, thro' the air. When it passes thro' dense bodies, 'tis unseen. When a wire makes part of the circle, in the explosion of the electrical phial, the fire, though in great quantity, passes in the wire invisibly: but in passing along a chain, it becomes visible as it leaps from link to link. In passing along leaf gilding 'tis visible: for the leaf gold is full of pores; hold a leaf to the light and it appears like a net, and the fire is seen in its leaping over the vacancies. And as when a long canal filled with still water is opened at one end, in order to be discharged, the motion of the water begins first near the opened end, and proceeds towards the close end, tho' the water itself moves from the close towards the opened end: so the electrical fire discharged into the polar regions, perhaps from a thousand leagues length of vaporised air, appears first where 'tis first in motion, *i.e.*, in the most northern part, and the appearance proceeds southward, tho' the fire really moves northward. This is supposed to account for the *Aurora Borealis*.

41. When there is great heat on the land, in a particular region (the sun having shone on it perhaps several days, while the surrounding countries have been screen'd by clouds) the lower air is rarified and rises, the cooler, denser air above descends; the clouds in that air meet from all sides, and join over the heated place; and if some are electrified, others not, lightning and thunder succeed, and showers fall. Hence thunder-gusts after heats, and cool air after gusts; the water and the clouds that bring it, coming from a higher and therefore a cooler region.

42. An electrical spark, drawn from an irregular body at some distance, is scarce ever strait, but shows crooked and waving in the air. So do the flashes of lightning, the clouds being very irregular bodies.

43. As electrified clouds pass over a country, high hills and high trees, lofty towers, spires, masts of ships, chimneys, &c., as so many prominencies and points, draw the electrical fire, and the whole cloud discharges there.

44. Dangerous, therefore, is it to take shelter under a tree, during a thunder-gust. It has been fatal to many, both men and beasts.

45. It is safer to be in the open field for another reason. When the cloaths are wet, if a flash in its way to the ground should strike your head, it may run in the water over the surface of your body; whereas, if your cloaths were dry, it would go through the body, [because the blood and other humours, containing so much water, are more ready conductors—1774].

Hence a wet rat cannot be killed by the exploding electrical bottle, when a dry rat may.[1]

---

[1] This was tried with a bottle, containing about a quart. It is since thought that one of the large glass jars, mentioned in these papers, might have killed him, though wet.

46. Common fire is in all bodies, more or less, as well as electrical fire. Perhaps they may be different modifications of the same element; or they may be different elements. The latter is by some suspected.

47. If they are different things, yet they may and do subsist together in the same body.

48. When electrical fire strikes through a body, it acts upon the common fire contained in it, and puts that fire in motion; and if there be a sufficient quantity of each kind of fire, the body will be inflamed.

49. When the quantity of common fire in the body is small, the quantity of the electrical fire (or the electrical stroke) should be greater: if the quantity of common fire be great, less electrical fire suffices to produce the effect.

50. Thus spirits must be heated before we can fire them by the electrical spark.[1] If they are much heated, a small spark will do; if not, the spark must be greater.

51. Till lately, we could only fire warm vapours; but now we can burn hard, dry rosin. And when we can procure greater electrical sparks, we may be able to fire not only unwarm'd spirits, as lightning does, but even wood, by giving sufficient agitation to the common fire contained in it, as friction we know will do.

52. Sulphureous and inflammable vapours arising from the earth, are easily kindled by lightning. Besides what arise from the earth, such vapours are sent out by stacks of moist hay, corn, or other vegetables, which heat and reek. Wood, rotting in old trees or buildings, does the same. Such are therefore easily and often fired.

53. Metals are often melted by lightning, tho' perhaps not from heat in the lightning, nor altogether from agitated fire in the metals. For as whatever body can insinuate itself between the particles of metal, and overcome the attraction by which they cohere (as sundry *menstrua* can) will make the solid become a fluid, as well as fire, yet without heating it: so the electrical fire, or lightning, creating a violent repul-

---

[1] We have since fired spirits without heating them, when the weather is warm. A little poured into the palm of the hand, will be warmed sufficiently by the hand, if the spirit be well rectified. Ether takes fire most readily.

sion between the particles of the metal it passes through, the metal is fused.

54. If you would, by a violent fire, melt off the end of a nail, which is half driven into a door, the heat given the whole nail before a part would melt, must burn the board it sticks in. And the melted part would burn the floor it dropp'd on. But if a sword can be melted in the scabbard, and money in a man's pocket by lightning, without burning either, it must be a cold fusion.[1]

55. Lightning rends some bodies. The electrical spark will strike a hole through a quire of strong paper.

56. If the source of lightning, assigned in this paper, be the true one, there should be little thunder heard at sea far from land. And accordingly some old sea-captains, of whom enquiry has been made, do affirm, that the fact agrees perfectly with the hypothesis; for that in crossing the great ocean, they seldom meet with thunder till they come into soundings; and that the islands far from the continent have very little of it. And a curious observer, who lived 13 years at *Bermudas*, says, there was less thunder there in that whole time, than he has sometimes heard in a month at *Carolina*.

To PETER COLLINSON. *September 1753*

In my former paper on this subject, wrote first in 1747, enlarged and sent to *England* in 1749, I considered the sea as the grand source of lightning, imagining its luminous appearance to be owing to electric fire, produc'd by friction between the particles of water and those of salt. Living far from the sea, I had then no opportunity of making experiments on the sea water, and so embraced this opinion too hastily.

For in 1750 and 1751, being occasionally on the seacoast, I found,

---

[1] These facts, though related in several accounts, are now doubted; since it has been observed that the parts of a bell-wire which fell on the floor being broken and partly melted by lightning, did actually burn into the boards. (See "Philos. Trans." Vol. LI. Part I.) and Mr. *Kinnersley* has found, that a fine iron wire, melted by Electricity, has had the same effect.

by experiments, that sea water in a bottle, tho' at first it would by agitation appear luminous, yet in a few hours it lost that virtue; *hence, and from this,* that I could not by agitating a solution of sea salt in water produce any light, I first began to doubt of my former hypothesis, and to suspect, that the luminous appearance in sea water must be owing to some other principles.

I then considered whether it were not possible, that the particles of air, being electrics *per se*, might, in hard gales of wind, by their friction against trees, hills, buildings, &c., as so many minute electric globes, rubbing against non-electric cushions, draw the electric fire from the earth, and that the rising vapours might receive that fire from the air, and by such means the clouds become electrified.

If this were so, I imagined that by forcing a constant violent stream of air against my prime conductor, by bellows, I should electrify it *negatively;* the rubbing particles of air drawing from it part of its natural quantity of the electric fluid. I accordingly made the experiment, but it did not succeed.

In *September* 1752, I erected an iron rod to draw the lightning down into my house, in order to make some experiments on it, with two bells to give notice when the rod should be electrify'd: a contrivance obvious to every electrician.

I found the bells rang sometimes when there was no lightning or thunder, but only a dark cloud over the rod; that sometimes, after a flash of lightning, they would suddenly stop; and, at other times, when they had not rang before, they would, after a flash, suddenly begin to ring; that the electricity was sometimes very faint, so that, when a small spark was obtain'd, another could not be got for some time after; at other times the sparks would follow extremely quick, and once I had a continual stream from bell to bell, the size of a crow-quill: Even during the same gust there were considerable variations.

In the winter following I conceived an experiment, to try whether the clouds were electrify'd *positively* or *negatively;* but my pointed rod, with its apparatus, becoming out of order, I did not refit it till towards the spring, when I expected the warm weather would bring on more frequent thunder-clouds.

The experiment was this: To take two phials; charge one of them with lightning from the iron rod, and give the other an equal charge by the electric glass globe, thro' the prime conductor: When charg'd, to place them on a table within three or four inches of each other, a small cork ball being suspended by a fine silk thread from the ceiling, so as it might play between the wires. If both bottles then were electrify'd *positively*, the ball, being attracted and repelled by one, must be also repell'd by the other. If the one *positively*, and the other *negatively*, then the ball would be attracted and repell'd alternatively by each, and continue to play between them as long as any considerable charge remained.

Being very intent on making this experiment, it was no small mortification to me, that I happened to be abroad during two of the greatest thunder-storms we had early in the spring, and, tho' I had given orders in my family, that, if the bells rang when I was from home, they should catch some of the lightning for me in electrical phials, and they did so, yet it was mostly dissipated before my return, and in some of the other gusts, the quantity of lightning I was able to obtain was so small, and the charge so weak, that I could not satisfy myself: Yet I sometimes saw what heighten'd my suspicions, and inflamed my curiosity.

At last, on the 12th of *April*, 1753, there being a smart gust of some continuance, I charg'd one phial pretty well with lightning, and the other equally, as near as I could judge, with electricity from my glass globe; and, having placed them properly, I beheld, with great surprize and pleasure, the cork ball play briskly between them, and was convinced, that one bottle was electrised *negatively*.

I repeated this experiment several times during the gust, and in eight succeeding gusts, always with the same success; and being of opinion (for reasons I formerly gave in my letter to Mr. *Kinnersley*, since printed in *London*), that the glass globe electrises *positively*, I concluded, that the clouds are *always* electrised *negatively*, or have always in them less than their natural quantity of the electric fluid.

Yet notwithstanding so many experiments, it seems I concluded too soon; for at last, *June* the 6th, in a gust which continued from five o'clock, P. M., to seven, I met with one cloud that was electrised *positively*, tho' several that pass'd over my rod before, during the same gust, were in the *negative* state. This was thus discovered:

I had another concurring experiment, which I often repeated, to prove the negative state of the clouds, *viz.*, While the bells were ringing, I took the phial charged from the glass globe, and applied its wire to the erected rod, considering, that if the clouds were electrised *positively*, the rod which received its electricity from them, must be so too; and then the additional *positive* electricity of the phial would make the bells ring faster:—But, if the clouds were in a *negative* state, they must exhaust the electric fluid from my rod, and bring that into the same negative state with themselves, and then the wire of a positively charg'd phial, supplying the rod with what it wanted (which it was obliged otherwise to draw from the earth by means of the pendulous brass ball playing between the two bells) the ringing would cease till the bottle was discharg'd.

In this manner I quite discharged into the rod several phials that were charged from the glass globe, the electric fluid streaming from the wire to the rod, 'till the wire would receive no spark from the finger; and during this supply to the rod from the phial, the bells stopt ringing; but by continuing the application of the phial wire to the rod, I exhausted the natural quantity from the inside surface of the same phials, or, as I call it, charged them *negatively*.

At length, while I was charging a phial by my glass globe, to repeat this experiment, my bells, of themselves, stopt ringing, and, after some pause, began to ring again. But now, when I approached the wire of the charg'd phial to the rod, instead of the usual stream that I expected from the wire to the rod, there was no spark;—not even when I brought the wire and the rod to touch; yet the bells continued ringing vigorously, which proved to me, that the rod was then *positively* electrify'd, as well as the wire of the phial, and equally so; and, consequently, that the particular cloud then over the rod, was in the same positive state. This was near the end of the gust.

But this was a single experiment, which, however, destroys my first too general conclusion, and reduces me to this: *That the clouds of a thunder-gust are most commonly in a negative state of electricity, but sometimes in a positive state.*

The latter I believe is rare; for, tho' I soon after the last experiment, set out on a journey to *Boston*, and was from home most part of the summer, which prevented my making farther trials and observations; yet Mr. *Kinnersley*, returning from the islands just as I left home, pursued the experiments during my absence, and informs me, that he always found the clouds in the *negative* state.

So that, for the most part, in thunder-strokes, *'tis the earth that strikes into the clouds, and not the clouds that strike into the earth.*

Those who are vers'd in electric experiments, will easily conceive, that the effects and appearances must be nearly the same in either case; the same explosion, and the same flash between one cloud and another, and between the clouds and mountains, &c., the same rending of trees, walls, &c., which the electric fluid meets with in its passage, and the same fatal shock to animal bodies; and that pointed rods fix'd on buildings, or masts of ships, and communicating with the earth or sea, must be of the same service in restoring the equilibrium silently between the earth and clouds, or in conducting a flash or stroke, if one should be, so as to save harmless the house or vessel: For points have equal power to throw off, as to draw on the electric fire, and rods will conduct up as well as down.

But tho' the light gained from these experiments makes no alteration in the practice, it makes a considerable one in the theory. And now we as much need an hypothesis to explain what means the clouds become negatively, as before to shew how they became positively electrified.

I cannot forbear venturing some few conjectures on this occasion: They are what occur to me at present, and, tho' future discoveries should prove them not wholly right, yet they may in the mean time be of some use, by stirring up the curious to make more experiments, and occasion more exact disquisitions.

I conceive then, that this globe of earth and water, with its plants, animals, and buildings, have, diffused throughout their substance, a quantity of the electric fluid, just as much as they can contain, which I call the *natural quantity.*

That this natural quantity is not the same in all kinds of common matter under the same dimensions, nor in the same kind of common matter in all circumstances; but a solid foot, for instance, of one kind of common matter, may contain more of the electric fluid than a solid foot of some other kind of common matter; and a pound weight of the same kind of common matter may, when in a rarer state, contain more of the electric fluid than when in a denser state.

For the electric fluid, being attracted by any portion of common matter, the parts of that fluid (which have among themselves a mutual repulsion) are brought so near to each other by the attraction of the common matter that absorbs them, as that their repulsion is equal to the condensing power of attraction in common matter; and then such portion of common matter will absorb no more.

Bodies of different kinds, having thus attracted and absorbed what I call their *natural quantity*, *i.e.* just as much of the electric fluid as is suited to their circumstances of density, rarity, and power of attracting, do not then show any signs of electricity among each other.

And if more electric fluid be added to one of these bodies, it does not enter, but spreads on the surface, forming an atmosphere; and then such body shews signs of electricity.

I have in a former paper compar'd common matter to a sponge, and the electric fluid to water: I beg leave once more to make use of the same comparison, to illustrate farther my meaning in this particular.

When a sponge is somewhat condens'd by being squeezed between the fingers, it will not receive and retain so much water as when in its more loose and open state.

If *more* squeez'd and condens'd, some of the water will come out of its inner parts, and flow on the surface.

If the pressure of the fingers be entirely removed, the sponge will not only resume what was lately forced out, but attract an additional quantity.

As the sponge in its rarer state will *naturally* attract and absorb *more* water, and in its denser state will *naturally* attract and absorb *less* water; we may call the quantity it attracts and absorbs in either state, its *natural quantity*, the state being considered.

Now what the sponge is to water, the same is water to the electric fluid.

When a portion of water is in its common dense state, it can hold no more electric fluid than it has; if any be added, it spreads on the surface.

When the same portion of water is rarefy'd into vapour, and forms a cloud, it is then capable of receiving and absorbing a much greater quantity; there is room for each particle to have an electric atmosphere.

Thus water, in its rarefy'd state, or in the form of a cloud, will be in a negative state of electricity; it will have less than its *natural quantity;* that is, less than it is naturally capable of attracting and absorbing in that state.

Such a cloud, then, coming so near the earth as to be within the striking distance, will receive from the earth a flash of the electric fluid; which flash, to supply a great extent of cloud, must sometimes contain a very great quantity of that fluid.

Or such a cloud, passing over woods of tall trees, may from the points and sharp edges of their moist top leaves, receive silently some supply.

A cloud, being by any means supply'd from the earth, may strike into other clouds that have not been supply'd, or not so much supply'd; and those to others, till an equilibrium is produc'd among all the clouds that are within striking distance of each other.

The cloud thus supply'd, having parted with much of what it first receiv'd, may require and receive a fresh supply from the earth, or from some other cloud, which, by the wind, is brought into such a situation as to receive it more readily from the earth.

Hence repeated and continual strokes and flashes till the clouds have all got nearly their natural quantity as clouds, or till they have descended in showers, and are united again with this terraqueous globe, their original.

Thus thunder-clouds are generally in a negative state of electricity compar'd with the earth, agreeable to most of our experiments; yet as by one experiment we found a cloud electris'd positively, I conjecture that, in that case, such cloud, after having received what was, in its rare state, only its *natural quantity*, became compress'd by the driving winds, or some other means, so that part of what it had absorb'd was forc'd out, and form'd an electric atmosphere around it in its denser state. Hence it was capable of communicating positive electricity to my rod.

To show that a body in different circumstances of dilatation and contraction is capable of receiving and retaining more or less of the electric fluid on its surface, I would relate the following experiment. I placed a clean wine-glass on the floor, and on it a small silver can. In the can I put about three yards of brass chain; to one end of which I fastened a silk thread, which went right up to the cieling, where it passed over a pulley, and came down again to my hand, that I might at pleasure draw the chain up out of the can, extending it till within a foot of the cieling, and let it gradually sink into the can again.— From the cieling, by another thread of fine raw silk, I suspended a small light lock of cotton, so as that when it hung perpendicularly, it came in contact with the side of the can.—Then approaching the wire of a charged vial to the can, I gave it a spark, which flow'd round in an electric atmosphere; and the lock of cotton was repelled from the side of the can to the distance of about nine or ten inches. The can would not then receive another spark from the wire of the vial; but, as I gradually drew up the chain, the atmosphere of the can diminish'd by flowing over the rising chain, and the lock of cotton accordingly drew nearer and nearer to the can; and then, if I again brought the vial wire near the can, it would receive another spark, and the cotton fly off again to its first distance; and thus, as the chain was drawn higher, the can would receive more sparks; because the can and extended chain were capable of supporting a greater atmosphere than the can with the chain gather'd up into its belly.—And that the atmosphere round the can was diminished by raising the chain, and increased again by lowering it, is not only agreeable to reason, since the atmosphere of the chain must be drawn from that of the can, when it rose, and returned to it again when it fell; but was also evident to the eye, the lock of cotton always approaching the can when the chain was drawn up, and receding when it was let down again.

Thus we see, that increase of surface makes a body capable of receiving a greater electric atmosphere: But this experiment does not, I own, fully demonstrate my new hypothesis; for the brass and silver still continue in their solid state, and are not rarefied into vapour, as the water is in clouds. Perhaps some future experiments on vapourized water may set this matter in a clearer light.

One seemingly material objection arises to the new hypothesis, and it is this. If water, in its rarefied state, as a cloud, requires and will absorb more of the electric fluid than when in its dense state as water, why does it not acquire from the earth all it wants at the instant of its leaving the surface, while it is yet near, and but just rising in vapour? To this difficulty I own I cannot at present give a solution satisfactory to myself: I thought, however, that I ought to state it in its full force as I have done, and submit the whole to examination.

And I would beg leave to recommend it to the curious in this branch of natural philosophy, to repeat with care and accurate observation the experiments I have reported in this and former papers relating to *positive* and *negative* electricity, with such other relative ones as shall occur to them, that it may be certainly known whether the electricity communicated by a glass globe be *really positive*. And also I would request all who may have an opportunity of observing the recent effects of lightning on buildings, trees, &c., that they would consider them particularly with a view to discover the direction. But in these examinations, this one thing is always to be understood, *viz.*, that, a stream of the electric fluid passing thro' wood, brick, metal, &c., while such fluid passes in *small quantity*, the mutually repulsive power of its parts is confined and overcome by the cohesion of the parts of the body it passes thro' so as to prevent an explosion; but, when the fluid comes in a quantity too great to be confined by such cohesion, it explodes, and rends or fuses the body that endeavoured to confine it. If it be wood, brick, stone, or the like, the splinters will flie off on that side where there is least resistance. And thus, when a hole is struck thro' pasteboard by the electrify'd jar, if the surfaces of the pasteboard are not confin'd or compress'd, there will be a bur rais'd all round the hole on both sides the pasteboard; but if one side be confin'd, so that the bur cannot be rais'd on that side, it will be all raised on the other; which way soever the fluid was directed. For the bur round the outside of the hole is the effect of the explosion every way from the center of the stream, and not an effect of the direction.

In every stroke of lightning, I am of opinion that the stream of the electric fluid, moving to restore the equilibrium between the cloud and the earth, does always previously find its passage, and mark out, as I may say, its own course, taking in its way all the conductors it can find, such as metals, damp walls, moist wood, &c., and will go considerably out of a direct course, for the sake of the assistance of good conductors; and that, in this course, it is actually moving, tho' silently and imperceptibly, before the explosion, in and among the conductors; which explosion happens only when the conductors cannot discharge it as fast as they receive it, by reason of their being incompleat, disunited, too small, or not of the best materials for conducting. Metalline rods, therefore, of sufficient thickness, and extending from the highest part of an edifice to the ground, being of the best materials and compleat conductors, will, I think, secure the building from damage, either by restoring the equilibrium so fast as to prevent a stroke, or by conducting it in the substance of the rod as far as the rod goes, so that there shall be no explosion but what is above its point between that and the clouds.

If it be ask'd, What thickness of a metalline rod may be suppos'd sufficient? in answer, I would remark, that five large glass jars, such as I have described in my former papers, discharge a very great quantity of electricity, which nevertheless will be all conducted round the corner of a book, by the fine filletting of gold on the cover, it following the gold the farthest way about, rather than take the shorter course through the cover, that not being so good a conductor. Now in this line of gold, the metal is so extremely thin as to be little more than the colour of gold, and on an octavo book is not in the whole an inch square, and therefore not the thirty-sixth part of a grain, according to M. *Réaumur;* yet 'tis sufficient to conduct the charge of five large jars, and how many more I know not. Now, I suppose a wire of a quarter an inch diameter to contain about 5000 times as much metal as there is in that gold line; and, if so, it will conduct the charge of 25,000 such glass jars, which is a quantity, I imagine, far beyond what was ever contain'd in any one stroke of natural lightning. But a rod of half an inch diameter would conduct four times as much as one of a quarter.

And with regard to conducting, tho' a certain thickness of metal be required to conduct a great quantity of electricity, and, at the same time, keep its own substance firm and unseparated; and a less quantity, as a very small wire for instance, will be destroyed by the explosion; yet such small wire will have answered the end of conducting that stroke, tho' it become incapable of conducting another. And considering the extream rapidity with which the electric fluid moves without exploding, when it has a free passage, or compleat metal communication, I should think a vast quantity would be conducted in a short time, either to or from a cloud, to restore its equilibrium with the earth, by means of a very small wire; and therefore thick rods should seem not so necessary.—However, as the quantity of lightning discharg'd in one stroke, cannot well be measured, and in different strokes is certainly very various, in some much greater than in others; and as iron (the best metal for the purpose, being least apt to fuse) is cheap, it may be well enough to provide a larger canal to guide that impetuous blast, than we imagine necessary: For, though one middling wire may be sufficient, two or three can do no harm. And time, with careful observations well compar'd, will at length point out the proper size to greater certainty.

Pointed rods erected on edifices may likewise often prevent a stroke, in the following manner. An eye so situated as to view horizontally the under side of a thunder-cloud, will see it very ragged, with a number of separate fragments, or petty clouds, one under another, the lowest sometimes not far from the earth. These, as so many stepping-stones, assist in conducting a stroke between the cloud and a building. To represent these by an experiment, take two or three locks of fine loose cotton, connect one of them with the prime conductor by a fine thread of two inches (which may be spun out of the same lock by the fingers), another to that, and the third to the second, by like threads. Turn the globe, and you will se these locks extend themselves towards the table (as the lower small clouds do towards the earth), being attracted by it: But on presenting a sharp point erect under the lowest, it will shrink up to the second, the second to the first, and all together to the prime conductor, where they will continue as long as the point continues under them. May not, in like manner, the small electrised clouds, whose equilibrium with the earth is soon restor'd by the point, rise up to the main body, and by that means occasion so large a vacancy, as that the grand cloud cannot strike in that place?

These thoughts, my dear friend, are many of them crude and hasty; and if I were merely ambitious of acquiring some reputation in philosophy, I ought to keep them by me, till corrected and improved by time and farther experience. But since even short hints and imperfect experiments in any new branch of science, being communicated, have oftentimes a good effect, in exciting the attention of the ingenious to the subject, and so become the occasion of more exact disquisition, and more compleat discoveries. You are at liberty to communicate this paper to whom you please; it being of more importance that knowledge should increase, than that your friend should be thought an accurate philosopher.

To PETER COLLINSON. *April 18, 1754*

Since *September* last, having been abroad on two long journeys, and otherwise much engag'd, I have made but few observations on the *positive* and *negative* state of electricity in the clouds. But Mr. *Kinnersley* kept his rod and bells in good order, and has made many.

Once this winter the bells rang a long time during a fall of snow, tho' no thunder was heard, or lightning seen. Sometimes the flashes and cracks of the electric matter between bell and bell were so large and loud as to be heard all over the house: but by all his observations, the clouds were constantly in a negative state, till about six weeks ago, when he found them once to change in a few minutes from the negative to the positive. About a fortnight after that he made another observation of the same kind; and last *Monday* afternoon, the wind blowing hard at S. E. and veering round to N. E., with many thick, driving clouds, there were five or six successive changes from negative to positive, and from positive to negative, the bells stopping a minute or two between every change. Besides the methods mentioned in my paper of *September* last, of discovering the electrical state of the clouds, the following may be us'd. When your bells are ringing, pass a rubb'd tube by the edge of the bell, connected with your pointed rod: if the cloud is then in a negative state, the ringing will stop; if in a positive state, it will continue, and perhaps be quicker. Or, suspend a very small cork ball by a fine silk thread, so that it may hang close to the edge of the rod-bell: then whenever the bell is electrified, whether positively or negatively, the little ball will be repell'd, and continue at some distance from the bell. Have ready a round-headed glass stopper of a decanter, rub it on your side till it is electrified, then present it to the cork ball. If the electricity in the ball is positive, it will be repell'd from the glass stopper, as well as from the bell; if negative, it will fly to the stopper.

(e) Superstitions Yesterday and Today

In the so-called age of enlightenment the majority of folks still had perpetual fear of the unleashing of natural forces like lightning and earthquakes. The historian pastor of Old South Church, Thomas Prince (1687–1758), gave a sermon in 1750 on "Earthquakes, the work of God," in which lightning was regarded as producing a series of earthquakes. In view of the disastrous Lisbon earthquake (1755) and a slight one in New England (1755), in that same year in the Harvard Chapel, Winthrop gave a "Lecture on earthquakes" as being "neither objections against the order of Providence, nor tokens of God's displeasure, but necessary consequences of natural laws." A paper war ensued. In Europe bells were often inscribed with the words *fulgura frango*" ("I break the lightning"). In 1784 Fisher of Munich completed a 33-year study of lightning; he found that 386 church towers has been struck and 103 bellringers killed. Even in 1787 the Paris Parliament had to renew Charlemagne's (768–814) edict against bell ringing in storms. Nevertheless, a hundred years ago bells were still being rung for this purpose.

The age of superstition, however, has not been wholly behind us. Many of us today still believe that lightning never strikes twice in the same place—despite the fact that the New York Empire State Building has been struck 68 times in three years—not to mention the Washington Monument.

Franklin had proposed the protective use of a lightning rod on July 29, 1750; in *Poor Richard, 1753*, he first published a description of "How to secure house, etc. from lightning." St. Paul's Cathedral had been struck in 1761 and 1767, as well as nearby St. Bride's in 1764; the former was protected with lightning rods in 1791. In 1769 the Roman town of Brescia in northern Italy lost one-sixth of its population when lightning struck a powder magazine; in 1772 the English magazine at Purfleet was struck. A committee of the Royal Society, including Franklin, recommended for protection pointed conductors in preference to ball-headed rods on buildings. Keen partisanship developed with George III siding with the lone dissenter Wilson (subsequently appointed to succeed William Hogarth (1697–1764) as Sergeant Painter to the Board of Ordnance). Pringle, President of the Royal Society and later (1774) physician to Queen Charlotte, resigned his presidency; he commented that the king "could not reverse the laws and operations of nature." Blunt rods soon appeared on Kew Palace and other government installations—and Purfleet was again struck a few years later despite the new Tory rods. A new Royal Society committee reported in favor of Franklin, then a "rebel." In France the revolutionaries Marat and Robespierre both approved pointed rods; in Italy, Pope Benedict XIV (1675–1758) had recommended them (they were used in some churches there). Abbé Nollet, however, contended that it was "as impious to ward off God's lightning as for a child to resist the chastening rod of the father."

Some people went about with unsheathed swords overhead to simulate lightning rods; clerics were obviously at a disadvantage. Both groups were partially right and wrong. Nollet was correct in that a cloud does not produce an appreciable inductive action on a point, and Wilson was right that, on the scale of the objects involved, a point was hardly distinguishable from a blunted object. The pointed rod, on the other hand, was definitely not harmful and decidedly protective if attached to a good grounding system. (An isolated tree or animal, including a human being, in the country affords an easier passage to the ground than a direct hit.)

Considerable attention was soon given to the protection of public buildings. Siena Cathedral, struck in 1771, was unharmed when lightning rods were properly installed. The New York Dutch Church was damaged in 1750 and in 1763, but, finally, had rods fixed in 1765. London St. Martin's in the Fields was unprotected in 1842 when it was struck. The Basilica of St. Mark's 325 ft campanile (c. 900) in Venice was no longer struck after rods had been properly erected—in contrast with its nine previous strikings (completely destroyed on three occasions).

Even more unusual, perhaps, are those historical buildings that have never been struck at all. Solomon's Temple (c. 900 BC) in Jerusalem had a roof covered with metal inside and outside, plus iron spikes for protection against birds and thieves—all connected by iron pipes to a cistern. The Roman Pantheon (first century A.D.) had a roof of bronze. St. Peter's Cathedral in Geneva had a wooden tower, but it was covered by tinned iron plate connected by metal to the ground. The 202 ft monument (c. 1675) in commemoration of the great London fire (1666) was protected by virtue of its pointed metal flame figures fixed to an iron base used as steps. The 984 ft metal Eiffel Tower (1889) is virtually a Faraday cage.

In the United State about 90 percent of the lightning strikes occur in the country. Nevertheless, 1300 persons are injured annually, and 500 killed—not to mention the considerable property loss each year. Yet only one-fifth of the US buildings that could profit thereby are protected from lightning.

Poor Richard Improved, 1753

RICHARD SAUNDERS, *Philadelphia, B. Franklin & D. Hall, 1752*

How to secure Houses, &c. from LIGHTNING

It has pleased God in his Goodness to Mankind, at length to discover to them the Means of securing their Habitations and other Buildings from Mischief by Thunder and Lightning. The Method is this: Provide a small Iron Rod (it may be made of the Rod-iron used by the Nailers) but of such a Length, that one End being three or four Feet in the moist Ground, the other may be six or eight Feet above the highest Part of the Building. To the upper End of the Rod fasten about a Foot of Brass Wire, the Size of a common Knitting-needle, sharpened to a fine Point; the Rod may be secured to the House by a few small Staples. If the House or Barn be long, there may be a Rod and Point at each End, and a middling Wire along the Ridge from one to the other. A House thus furnished will not be damaged by Lightning, it being attracted by the Points, and passing thro the Metal into the Ground without hurting any Thing. Vessels also, having a sharp pointed Rod fix'd on the Top of their Masts, with a Wire from the Foot of the Rod reaching down, round one of the Shrouds, to the Water, will not be hurt by Lightning.

CHAPTER 9

Handiwork

(a) Fireplaces

Franklin invented a fireplace in 1742 and described it in a special pamphlet he printed in 1744. (The iron plates for it were manufactured by Robert Grace (1709–66).) He declined an offer of the Pennsylvania deputy governor, George Thomas (*c*. 1695–1776), to patent it on the basis of the following principle: "That as we enjoy great advantages from the inventions of others, we should be glad of an opportunity to serve others by any invention of ours, and this we should do freely and generously." Franklin utilized all methods of heat transfer: primarily convection by having fresh air enter through a duct at the bottom, heated in an air box, and forced out of vents at the top; convection and radiation from the metal plates, and to a less degree conduction, owing to their direct contact with the air in the room. The later so-called Franklin stove eliminated the air box and was reduced essentially to a fireplace with metal plates instead of stone. Franklin continued his interest in heating devices throughout his life. For example, in 1785 he wrote a long letter to Ingenhousz "On the causes and cure of smoky chimneys." He utilized what we now call a damper in the chimney.

An account of the New Invented Pennsylvanian Fire-Places, 1744

6. Charcoal Fires, in Pots, are us'd chiefly in the Shops of Handicraftsmen. They warm a Room (that is kept close and has no Chimney to carry off the warm'd Air,) very speedily and uniformly: But there being no Draught to change the Air, the sulphurous Fumes from the Coals (be they ever so well kindled before they are brought in, there

will be some) mix with it, render it disagreeable, hurtful to some Constitutions, and sometimes, when the Door is long kept shut, produce fatal consequences.

To avoid the several Inconveniences, and at the same time retain all the Advantages of other Fire-places, was contrived the PENNSYL-VANIA FIRE-PLACE, now to be described.

This Machine consists of

A Bottom Plate, (i) (See Plate V.)—

A Back Plate, (ii)

Two Side Plates, (iii, iii)

Two Middle Plates, (iv, iv) which, join'd together form a tight Box with winding Passages in it for warming the Air.

A Front Plate, (v)

A Top Plate, (vi)

These are all of cast Iron, with Mouldings or Ledges where the Plates come together, to hold them fast, and retain the Mortar us'd for Pointing to make tight Joints. When the Plates are all in their Places, a Pair of slender Rods with Screws, are sufficient to bind the Whole very firmly together, as it appears in Fig. 2.

There are, moreover, two thin Plates of wrought Iron, *viz.* the Shutter (vii) and the Register (viii); besides the Screw-Rods, *O, P*, all which we shall explain in their Order.

(i) The Bottom Plate, or Hearth-Piece, is round before, with a rising Moulding, that serves as a Fender to keep Coals and Ashes from coming to the Floor, &c. It has two Ears, *F, G*, perforated to receive the Screw-Rods, *O P*; a long Air-Hole, *a a*, thro' which the fresh outward Air passes up into the Air-Box; and three Smoke-Holes, *B C* thro' which the Smoke descends and passes away; all represented by dark Squares. It has also double Ledges to receive between them the Bottom Edges of the Back Plate, the two Side Plates, and the two Middle Plates. These Ledges are about an Inch asunder, and about half an Inch high; a Profile of two of them, join'd to a Fragment of Plate, appears in Fig. 3.

(ii) The Back Plate is without Holes, having only a Pair of Ledges on each Side, to receive the Back Edges of the two.

Plate V.

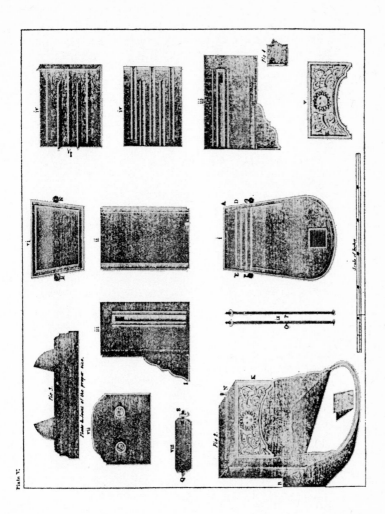

Plate & front of the proper size.

Scale of Inches

(iii, iii) Side Plates: These have each a Pair of Ledges to receive the Side Edges of the Front Plate, and a little Shoulder for it to rest on; also two Pair of Ledges to receive the Side Edges of the two Middle Plates, which form the Air-Box; and an oblong Air-hole near the Top, thro' which is discharged into the Room the Air warm'd in the Air-Box. Each has also a Wing or Bracket, *H* and *I*, to keep in falling Brands, Coals, &c., and a small Hole, *Q* and *R*, for the Axis of the Register to turn in.

(iv, iv) The Air-Box is compos'd of the two Middle Plates, *D E* and *F G*. The first has five thin Ledges or Partitions, cast on it, two Inches deep, the Edges of which are receiv'd in so many Pair of Ledges cast in the other. The Tops of all the Cavities form'd by these thin deep Ledges are also covered by a Ledge of the same Form and Depth, cast with them; so that when the Plates are put together, and the Joints luted, there is no Communication between the Air-Box and the Smoke. In the winding Passages of this Box, fresh Air is warm'd as it passes into the Room.

(v) The Front Plate is arch'd on the under Side, and ornamented with Foliages, &c.; it has no Ledges.

(vi) The Top Plate has a Pair of Ears, *M N*, answerable to those in the Bottom Plate, and perforated for the same Purpose: It has also a Pair of Ledges running round the under Side, to receive the Top Edges of the Front, Back, and Side Plates. The Air-Box does not reach up to the Top Plate by two Inches and half.

(vii) The Shutter is of thin wrought Iron and light, of such a Length and Breadth as to close well the Opening of the Fire-place. It is us'd to blow up the Fire, and to shut up and secure it a Nights. It has two brass Knobs for Handles, *d d*, and commonly slides up and down in a Groove, left, in putting up the Fire-place, between the foremost Ledge of the Side Plates, and the Face of the Front Plate; but some choose to set it aside when it is not in Use, and apply it on Occasion.

(viii) The Register, is also of thin wrought Iron. It is plac'd between the Back Plate and Air-Box, and can, by Means of the Key *S* be turn'd on its Axis so as to lie in any Position between level and upright.

The Screw-Rods, *O P* are of wrought Iron, about a third of an Inch thick, with a Button at Bottom, and a Screw and Nut at Top; and may be ornamented with two small Brasses screw'd on above the Nuts.

To put this Machine to work,

1. A false Back of four Inch—(or, in shallow small Chimneys, two-Inch—) Brick-Work is to be made in the Chimney, four Inches or more from the true Back: From the Top of this false Back, a Closing is to be made over to the Breast of the Chimney, that no Air may pass into the Chimney, but what goes under the false Back, and up behind it.

2. Some Bricks of the Hearth are to be taken up, to form a Hollow under the Bottom Plate; across which Hollow runs a thin tight Partition, to keep apart the Air entring the Hollow, and the Smoke; and is therefore plac'd between the Air-hole and Smoke-holes.

3. A Passage is made, communicating with the outward Air, to introduce that Air into the fore part of the Hollow under the Bottom Plate, whence it may rise thro' the Air-hole into the Air-box.

4. A Passage is made from the back Part of the Hollow, communicating with the Flue behind the false Back: Through this Passage the Smoke is to pass.

The Fire-place is to be erected upon these Hollows, by putting all the Plates in their Places, and screwing them together.

Its Operation may be conceiv'd by observing the Plate entitled, *Profile of the Chimney and Fire-place*. (See Plate VI.)

M The Mantle-piece, or Breast of the Chimney.

C The Funnel.

B The false Back and Closing.

E True Back of the Chimney.

T Top of the Fire-place.

F The Front of it.

A The Place where the Fire is made.

D The Air-Box.

K The Hole in the Side plate, thro' which the warm'd Air is discharg'd out of the Air-Box into the Room.

H The Hollow fill'd with fresh Air, entring at the Passage *I*, and

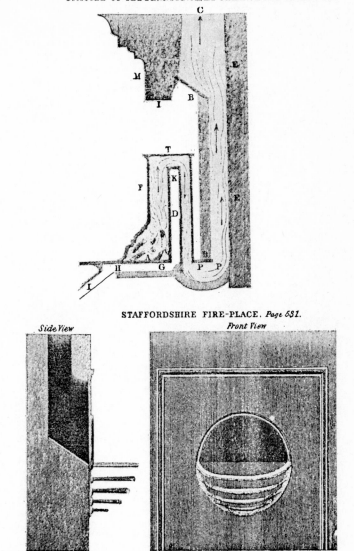

PROFILE OF THE PENNSYLVANIA CHIMNEY AND FIRE-PLACE

STAFFORDSHIRE FIRE-PLACE. *Page 581.*

Side View

Front View

PLATE VI

ascending into the Air-Box thro' the Air-hole in the Bottom plate, near

  G The Partition in the Hollow to keep the Air and Smoke apart.

  P The Passage under the false Back and Part of the Hearth for the Smoke.

  [The arrows show] the Course of the Smoke.

  The Fire being made at *A*, the Flame and Smoke will ascend and strike the Top *T*, which will thereby receive a considerable Heat. The Smoke, finding no Passage upwards, turns over the Top of the Air-box, and descends between it and the Back Plate to the Holes in the Bottom Plate, heating, as it passes, both Plates of the Air-box, and the said Back Plate; the Front Plate, Bottom and Side Plates are also all heated at the same Time. The Smoke proceeds in the Passage that leads it under and behind the false Back, and so rises into the Chimney. The Air of the Room, warm'd behind the Back Plate, and by the Sides, Front, and Top Plates, becoming specifically lighter than the other Air in the Room, is oblig'd to rise; but the Closure over the Fire-place hindring it from going up the Chimney, it is forc'd out into the Room, rises by the Mantle-piece to the Cieling, and spreads all over the Top of the Room, whence being crouded down gradually by the Stream of newly-warm'd Air that follows and rises above it, the whole Room becomes in a short time equally warmed.

  At the same Time the Air, warmed under the Bottom Plate and in the Air-Box, rises, and comes out of the Holes in the Side Plates, very swiftly if the Door of the Room be shut, and joins its Current with the Stream before mentioned, rising from the Side, Back, and Top Plates.

  The Air that enters the Room thro' the Air-box is fresh, tho' warm; and computing the Swiftness of its Notion with the Areas of the Holes, 'tis found that near 10 Barrels of fresh Air are hourly introduc'd by the Air-Box; and by this Means the Air in the Room is continually changed, and kept at the same Time sweet and warm.

  'Tis to be observed, that the entring Air will not be warm at first Lighting the Fire, but heats gradually as the Fire encreases.

  A square Opening for a Trap-Door should be left in the Closing of the Chimney, for the Sweeper to go up: The Door may be made of

Slate or Tin, and commonly kept close shut, but so plac'd as that turning up against the Back of the Chimney when open, it closes the Vacancy behind the false Back, and shoots the Soot, that falls in Sweeping, out upon the Hearth. This Trap-Door is a very convenient Thing.
, In Rooms where much Smoking of Tobacco is used, 'tis also convenient to have a small Hole, about five or six Inches square, cut near the Cieling through into the Funnel: This Hole must have a Shutter, by which it may be clos'd or open'd at Pleasure. When open, there will be a strong Draught of Air through it into the Chimney, which will presently carry off a Cloud of Smoke, and keep the Room clear: If the Room be too hot likewise, it will carry off as much of the warm Air as you please, and then you may stop it intirely, or in part, as you think fit. By this Means it is that the Tobacco Smoke does not descend among the Heads of the Company near the Fire, as it must do before it can get into common Chimneys.

The Manner of using this Fire-place

Your Cord-wood must be cut into three Lengths; or else a short Piece, fit for the Fire-place, cut off, and the longer left for the Kitchen or other Fires. Dry Hickery, or Ash, or any Woods that burn with a clear Flame, are rather to be chosen, because such are less apt to foul the Smoke Passages with Soot; and Flame communicates with its Light, as well as by Contact, greater Heat to the Plates and Room. But where more ordinary Wood is used, half a dry Faggot of Brushwood burnt at the first making of Fire in the Morning, is very advantageous; as it immediately by its sudden Blaze heats the Plates and warms the Room (which with bad Wood slowly kindling would not be done so soon) and at the same time, by the Length of its Flame turning in the Passages, consumes and cleanses away the Soot that such bad smoaky Wood had produc'd therein the preceding Day, and so keeps them always free and clean. When you have laid a little Back log, and plac'd your Billets on small Dogs, as in common Chimneys, and put some Fire to them, then slide down your Shutter as low as the Dogs, and the Opening being by that means contracted, the Air rushes in briskly and presently blows up the Flames. When the Fire is sufficiently kindled, slide it up again.[1] In some of these Fire-places there is a little six inch square Trap-door of thin wrought Iron or Brass, covering a Hole of like Dimensions near the Fore part of the Bottom Plate, which being by a Ring lifted up towards the Fire, about an Inch, where it will be retain'd by two springing Sides fix'd to it perpendicularly, (see Plate V., Fig. 4), the Air rushes in from the Hollow under the Bottom Plate, and blows the Fire. Where this is us'd, the Shutter serves only to close the Fire a Nights. The more forward you can make your Fire on the Hearth-Plate, not to be incommoded by the Smoke, the sooner and more will the Room be warmed. At Night, when you go to Bed, cover the Coals or Brands with Ashes as usual; then take away the Dogs, and slide down the Shutter close to the Bottom Plate, weeping a little Ashes against it that no Air may pass under it; then turn the Register, so as very near to stop the Flue behind. If no Smoke then comes out at Crevices into the Room, 'tis right: If any Smoke is perceiv'd to come out, move the Register so as to give a little Draught, and 'twill go the right way. Thus the Room will be kept warm all Night; for the Chimney being almost entirely stopt, very little, if any, cold Air will enter the Room at any Crevice. When you come to re-kindle the Fire in the Morning, turn open the Register before you lift up the Slider, otherwise if there be any Smoke in the Fire-Place, it will come out into the Room. By the same Use of the Shutter and Register, a blazing Fire may be presently stifled, as well as secured, when you have Occasion to leave it for any Time; and at your Return you will find the Brands warm, and ready for a speedy Re-kindling. The Shutter alone will not stifle a Fire; for it cannot well be made to fit so exactly

[1] The Shutter is slid up and down in this Manner, only in those Fire-places which are so made, as that the Distance between the Top of the arch'd Opening and the Bottom Plate is the same as the Distance between it and the Top Plate. Where the Arch is higher, as it is in the Draught annex'd (which is agreeable to the last Improvements), the Shutter is set by, and apply'd occasionally: because, if it were made deep enough to close the whole Opening when slid down, it would hide Part of it when up.

but that Air will enter, and that in a violent Stream, so as to blow up and keep alive the Flames, and consume the Wood, if the Draught be not check'd by turning the Register to shut the Flue behind. The Register has also two other Uses. If you observe the Draught of Air into your Fire-place to be stronger than is necessary (as in extream cold Weather it often is) so that the Wood is consum'd faster than usual; in that Case, a quarter, half, or two-thirds Turn of the Register, will check the Violence of the Draught, and let your Fire burn with the Moderation you desire: And at the same Time both the Fire-Place and the Room will be the warmer, because less cold Air will enter and pass through them. And if the Chimney should happen to take Fire (which indeed there is very little Danger of, if the preceding Direction be observ'd in making Fires, and it be well swept once a Year; for, much less Wood being burnt, less Soot is proportionably made; and the Fuel being soon blown into Flame by the Shutter, (or the Trap-door Bellows) there is consequently less Smoke from the Fuel to make Soot; then, tho' the Funnel should be foul, yet the Sparks have such a crooked up and down round-about Way to go, that they are out before they get at it) I say, if ever it should be on fire, a Turn of the Register shuts all close, and prevents any Air going into the Chimney, and so the Fire may easily be stifled and mastered.

The Advantages of this Fire-place

Its Advantages above the common Fire-places are,

1. That your whole Room is equally warmed; so that People need not croud so close round the Fire, but may sit near the Window, and have the Benefit of the Light for Reading, Writing, Needlework, &c. They may sit with Comfort in any Part of the Room, which is a very considerable Advantage in a large Family, where there must often be two Fires kept, because all cannot conveniently come at one.

2. If you sit near the Fire, you have not that cold Draught of uncomfortable Air nipping your Back and Heels, as when before common Fires, by which many catch Cold, being scorcht before, and, as it were, froze behind.

3. If you sit against a Crevice, there is not that sharp Draught of cold Air playing on you, as in Rooms where there are Fires in the common way; by which many catch Cold, whence proceed Coughs,[1] Catarrhs, Tooth-achs, Fevers, Pleurisies, and many other Diseases.

4. In Case of Sickness, they make most excellent Nursing-Rooms; as they constantly supply a Sufficiency of fresh Air, so warmed at the same time as to be no way inconvenient or dangerous. A small One does well in a Chamber; and, the Chimneys being fitted for it, it may be remov'd from one Room to another, as Occasion requires, and fix'd in half an Hour. The equal Temper, too, and Warmth, of the Air of the Room, is thought to be particularly advantageous in some Distempers: For 'twas observ'd in the Winters of 1730 and 1736, when the Small-Pox spread in *Pennsylvania,* that very few of the Children of the *Germans* died of that Distemper in Proportion to those of the *English;* which was ascrib'd by some to the Warmth and equal Temper of Air in their Stove-Rooms; which made the Disease as favourable as it commonly is in the *West Indies.* But this Conjecture we submit to the judgment of Physicians.

5. In common Chimneys, the strongest Heat from the Fire, which is upwards, goes directly up the Chimney, and is lost; and there is such a strong Draught into the Chimney, that not only the upright Heat, but also the back, sides, and downward Heats are carried up the Chimney by that Draught of Air; and the Warmth given before the Fire, by the Rays that strike out towards the Room, is continually driven back, crouded into the Chimney, and carried up, by the same Draught of Air. But here the upright Heat strikes and heats the Top Plate, which warms the Air above it, and that comes into the Room. The Heat likewise, which the Fire communicates to the Sides, Back Bottom and Air-Box, is all brought into the Room; for you will find

---

[1] My Lord *Molesworth,* in his account of *Denmark,* says, "That few or none of the People there are troubled with Coughs, Catarrhs, Consumptions, or such like Diseases of the Lungs; so that in the Midst of Winter in the Churches, which are very much frequented, there is no Noise to interrupt the Attention due to the Preacher. I am persuaded" (says he) "their *warm Stoves* contribute to their Freedom from these kinds of Maladies," page 91.

a constant Current of warm Air coming out of the Chimney-Corner into the Room. Hold a Candle just under the Mantle-Piece, or Breast of your Chimney, and you will see the Flame bent outwards: By laying a Piece of Smoaking Paper on the Hearth, on either Side, you may see how the Current of Air moves, and where it tends, for it will turn and carry the Smoke with it.

6. Thus, as very little of the Heat is lost, when this Fire-Place is us'd, *much less Wood*[1] will serve you, which is a considerable Advantage where Wood is dear.

7. When you burn Candles near this Fire-Place, you will find that the Flame burns quite upright, and does not blare and run the Tallow down, by drawing towards the Chimney, as against common Fires.

8. This Fire-place cures most smoaky chimneys, and thereby preserves both the Eyes and Furniture.

9. It prevents the Fouling of Chimneys; much of the Lint and Dust that contributes to foul a Chimney, being by the low Arch oblig'd to pass thro' the Flame, where 'tis consum'd. Then, less Wood being burnt, there is less Smoke made. Again, the Shutter, or Trap-Bellows, soon blowing the Wood into a Flame, the same Wood does not yield so much Smoke as if burnt in a common Chimney: For as soon as Flame begins, Smoke, in proportion, ceases.

10. And, if a Chimney should be foul, 'tis much less likely to take Fire. If it should take Fire, 'tis easily stifled and extinguished.

11. A Fire may be very speedily made in this Fire-Place, by the Help of the Shutter, or Trap-Bellows, as aforesaid.

12. A Fire may be soon extinguished by closing it with the Shutter

---

[1] People, who have us'd these Fire-places, differ much in their Accounts of the Wood saved by them. Some say five sixths, others three fourths, and others much less. This is owing to the great Difference there was in their former Fires; some (according to the different Circumstances of their Rooms and Chimneys) having been us'd to make very large, others middling, and others, of a more sparing Temper, very small Ones. While in these Fire-Places (their Size and Draught being nearly the same) the Consumption is more equal. I suppose, taking a Number of Families together, that two thirds, or half the Wood, at least, is saved. My common Room, I know, is made twice as warm as it used to be, with a quarter of the Wood I formerly consum'd there.

before, and turning the Register behind, which will stifle it, and the Brands will remain ready to rekindle.

13. The Room being once warm, the Warmth may be retain'd in it all Night.

14. And lastly, the Fire is so secur'd at Night, that not one Spark can fly out into the Room to do Damage.

With all these Conveniencies, you do not lose the pleasing Sight nor Use of the Fire, as in the Dutch Stoves, but may boil the Tea-Kettle, warm the Flat-Irons, heat Heaters, keep warm a Dish of Victuals by setting it on the Top, &c. &c.

There are some Objections commonly made by People that are unacquainted with these Fire-Places, which it may not be amiss to endeavour to remove, as they arise from Prejudices which might otherwise obstruct in some Degree the general Use of this beneficial Machine. We frequently hear it said, *They are of the Nature of Dutch Stoves; Stoves have an unpleasant Smell; Stoves are unwholesome; and Warm Rooms make People tender, and apt to catch Cold.* As to the first, that they are of the Nature of *Dutch* Stoves, the Description of those Stoves in the Beginning of this Paper, compar'd with that of these Machines, shows that there is a most material Difference, and that these have vastly the Advantage, if it were only in the single Article of the Admission and Circulation of fresh Air. But it must be allowed there may have been some Cause to complain of the offensive Smell of Iron Stoves. This Smell, however, never proceeded from the Iron itself, which in its Nature, whether hot or cold, is one of the sweetest of Metals, but from the general uncleanly Manner of using those Stoves. If they are kept clean, they are as sweet as an Ironing-Box, which, tho' ever so hot, never offends the Smell of the nicest Lady; but it is common to let them be greased by setting Candle-sticks on them, or otherwise; to rub greasy Hands on them, and, above all, to spit upon them to try how hot they are, which is an inconsiderate, filthy unmannerly Custom; for the slimy Matter of Spittle drying on, burns and fumes when the Stove is hot, as well as the Grease, and smells most nauseously; which makes such close Stove-Rooms, where there is no Draught to carry off those filthy

Vapours, almost intolerable to those that are not from their Infancy accustomed to them. At the same time, nothing is more easy than to keep them clean; for when by any Accident they happen to be fouled, a Lee made of Ashes and Water, with a Brush, will scour them perfectly; as will also a little strong Soft Soap and Water.

That hot Iron of itself gives no offensive Smell, those know very well who have (as the Writer of this has) been present at a Furnace when the Workmen were pouring out the flowing Metal to cast large Plates, and not the least Smell of it to be perceived. That hot Iron does not, like Lead, Brass, and some other Metals, give out unwholesome Vapours, is plain from the general Health and Strength of those who constantly work in Iron, as Furnace-men, Forge-men, and Smiths; That it is in its Nature a Metal Perfectly wholesome to the Body of Man, is known from the beneficial Use of Chalybeat or Iron-Mine Waters; from the Good done by taking Steel Filings in several Disorders; and that even the Smithy Water, in which hot Irons are quench'd, is found advantageous to the human Constitution. The ingenious and learned Dr. *Desaguliers*, to whose instructive Writings the Contriver of this Machine acknowledges himself much indebted, relates an Experiment he made, to try whether heated Iron would yield unwholesome Vapours. He took a Cube of Iron, and having given it a very great Heat, he fix'd it so to a Receiver, exhausted by the Air-Pump, that all the Air rushing in to fill the Receiver, should first pass thro' a Hole in the hot Iron. He then put a small Bird into the Receiver, who breath'd that Air without any Inconvenience, or suffering the least Disorder. But the same Experiment being made with a Cube of hot Brass, a Bird put into that Air dy'd in a few Minutes. Brass, indeed, stinks even when cold, and much more when hot; Lead too, when hot, yields a very unwholesome Steam; but Iron is always sweet, and every way taken is wholesome and friendly to the human Body,—except in Weapons.

That warm Rooms make People tender and apt to catch Cold, is a Mistake as great as it is (among the *English*) general. We have seen in the preceding Pages how the common Rooms are apt to give Colds; but the Writer of this Paper may affirm, from his own Experience, and that of his Family and Friends who have used warm Rooms for these four Winters past, that by the Use of such Rooms, People are rendered *less liable* to take Cold, and, indeed, *actually hardened*. If sitting warm in a Room made One subject to take Cold on going out, lying warm in Bed should, by a Parity of Reason, produce the same Effect when we rise. Yet we find we can leap out of the warmest Bed naked in the coldest Morning, without any such Danger; and in the same Manner out of warm Clothes into a cold Bed. The Reason is, that in these Cases the Pores all close at once, the Cold is shut out, and the Heat within augmented, as we soon after feel by the glowing of the Flesh and Skin. Thus, no one was ever known to catch Cold by the use of the Cold Bath: And are not cold Baths allowed to harden the Bodies of those that use them? Are they not therefore frequently prescrib'd to the tenderest Constitutions? Now, every Time you go out of a warm Room into the cold freezing Air, you do as it were plunge into a Cold Bath, and the Effect is in proportion the same; for (tho' perhaps you may feel somewhat chilly at first) you find in a little Time your Bodies hardened and strengthened, your Blood is driven round with a brisker Circulation, and a comfortable, steady, uniform inward Warmth succeeds that equal outward Warmth you first received in the Room. Farther to confirm this Assertion, we instance the *Swedes*, the *Danes*, the *Russians;* these Nations are said to live in Rooms, compar'd to ours, as hot as Ovens;[1] yet where are the hardy Soldiers, tho' bred in their boasted cool Houses, that can, like

[1] Mr. *Boyle*, in his Experiments and Observations upon Cold, *Shaw's Abridgment*, Vol. I, p. 684, says, " 'Tis remarkable, that, while the Cold has strange and tragical Effects at Moscow and elsewhere, the *Russians* and *Livonians* should be exempt from them, who accustom themselves to pass immediately from a great Degree of Heat, to as great on one of Cold, without receiving any visible Prejudice thereby. I remember, being told by a Person of unquestionable Credit, that it was a common Practice among them, to go from a hot Stove into cold Water; the same was, also, affirmed to me by another who resided at *Moscow*. This Tradition is likewise abundantly confirmed by *Olearius*." " 'Tis a surprising thing," says he, "to see how far the Russians can endure Heat; and how, when it makes them ready to faint, they can go out of their Stoves, stark naked, both Men and Women, and throw themselves into cold Water, and even in Winter wallow in the Snow."

these People, bear the Fatigues of a Winter Campaign in so severe a Climate, march whole Days to the Neck in Snow, and at Night entrench in Ice, as they do?

The Mentioning of those Northern Nations puts me in Mind of a considerable *Publick Advantage* that may arise from the general Use of these Fire-places. It is observable, that tho' those Countries have been well inhabited for many Ages, Wood is still their Fuel, and yet at no very great Price; which could not have been if they had not universally used Stoves, but consum'd it as we do in great Quantities, by open Fires. By the Help of this saving Invention our Wood may grow as fast as we consume it, and our Posterity may warm themselves at a moderate Rate, without being oblig'd to fetch their Fuel over the *Atlantick;* as, if Pit-Coal should not be here discovered (which is an Uncertainty) they must necessarily do.

We leave it to the *Political Arithmetician* to compute how much Money will be sav'd to a Country, by its spending two thirds less of Fuel; how much Labour saved in Cutting and Carriage of it; how much more Land may be clear'd for Cultivation; how great the Profit by the additional Quantity of Work done, in those Trades particularly that do not exercise the Body so much, but that the Workfolks are oblig'd to run frequently to the Fire to warm themselves: And to physicians to say, how much healthier thick-built Towns and Cities will be, now half suffocated with sulphury Smoke, when so much less of that Smoke shall be made, and the Air breath'd by the Inhabitants be consequently so much purer. These Things it will suffice just to have mentioned; let us proceed to give some necessary Directions to the Workman, who is to fix or set up these Fire-Places.

(b) Musical Glasses

Since the beginning of time man has been fascinated by the sounds of vibrating bodies. In his *Two New Sciences* (1638) Galileo Galilei (1564–1642) mentioned the musical tone produced by rubbing one's finger tip along the rim of a goblet partially filled with water.

Concerts were given about 1741 with a set of tuned glasses by

Richard Pockrich (Puckeridge?, 1714–82). The German opera compos-
er Christoph Willibald von Gluck (1714–87) used them for a concert
in London, 1746. The musical glasses became quite popular there
about 1760.

Franklin improved the set up by having thirty-seven (three octaves)
self-tuned glass basins on a spindle operated with a pedal. Later a
keyboard was provided; in 1823 an instrument was made with 120
glasses.

Distinguished musicians gave serious attention to the so-called
(h)armonica. The fading sounds created a melancholy mood. The
Austrian Wolfgang Amadeus Mozart (1756–91), who himself played
it in Vienna at 17, composed an Adagio (K. 356) and Adagio and
Rondo (K. 617) for the blind girl Marianna Kirchgessner. The German
Ludwig van Beethoven (1770–1824) wrote an armonica accompaniment
as part of some incidental music. The armonica, however, was ex-
pensive and difficult to play—as well as breakable.

To GIAMBATISTA BECCARI. *July 13, 1762*

I once promised myself the pleasure of seeing you at *Turin;* but as
that is not now likely to happen, being just about returning to my
native country, *America,* I sit down to take leave of you (among
others of my *European* friends that I cannot see) by writing

I thank you for the honourable mention you have so frequently
made of me in your letters to Mr. *Collinson* and others, for the generous defence you undertook and executed with so much success, of
my electrical opinions; and for the valuable present you have made
me of your new work, from which I have received great information
and pleasure. I wish I could in return entertain you with any thing
new of mine on that subject; but I have not lately pursued it. Nor
do I know of any one here, that is at present much engaged in it.

Perhaps, however, it may be agreeable to you, as you live in a
musical country, to have an account of the new instrument lately
added here to the great number that charming science was before

possessed of: As it is an instrument that seems peculiarly adapted to *Italian* musci, especially that of the soft and plaintive kind, I will endeavour to give you such a description of it, and of the manner of constructing it, that you, or any of your friends may be enabled to imitate it, if you incline so to do, without being at the expence and trouble of the many experiments I have made in endeavouring to bring it to its present perfection.

You have doubtless heard the sweet tone that is drawn from a drinking-glass, by passing a wet finger round its brim. One Mr. *Puckeridge*,[1] a gentleman from *Ireland*, was the first who thought of playing tunes, formed of these tones. He collected a number of glasses of different sizes, fixed them near each other on a table, and tuned them by putting into them water, more or less each note required. The tones were brought out by passing his fingers round their brims. He was unfortunately burnt here, with his instrument, in a fire which consumed the house he lived in. Mr. E. *Delaval*,[2] a most ingenious member of our Royal Society, made one in imitation of it, with a better choice and form of glasses, which was the first I saw or heard. Being charmed by the sweetness of its tones, and the music he produced from it, I wished only to see the glasses disposed in a more convenient form, and brought together in a narrower compass, so as to admit of a greater number of tunes, and all within reach of hand to a person sitting before the instrument, which I accomplished, after various intermediate trials, and less commodious forms, both of glasses and construction, in the following manner.

The glasses are blown as near as possible in the form of hemispheres, having each an open neck or socket in the middle. (See Plate, Figure 1.) The thickness of the glass near the brim about a tenth of an inch, or hardly quite so much, but thicker as it comes nearer the neck, which in the largest glasses is about an inch deep, and an inch

---

[1] Richard Puckeridge, or Pockrich, inventor of the musical glasses. He died in 1759, about seventy years of age. — ED.

[2] Edmund Hussey Delaval (1729–1814), F.R.S., gave an account of the effects of lightning on St. Bride's Church, and was associated with Franklin in the commission to report on the protection of St. Paul's from lightning. — ED.

and half wide within, these dimensions lessening as the glasses themselves diminish in size, except that the neck of the smallest ought not to be shorter than half an inch. The largest glass is nine inches diameter, and the smallest three inches. Between these there are twenty-three different sizes, differing from each other a quarter of an inch in diameter. To make a single instrument there should be at least six glasses blown of each size; and out of this number one may probably pick 37 glasses, (which are sufficient for three octaves with all the semitones) that will be each either the note one wants or a little sharper than that note, and all fitting so well into each other as to taper pretty regularly from the largest to the smallest. It is true there are not 37 sizes, but it often happens that two of the same size differ a note or half note in tone, by reason of a difference in thickness, and these may be placed one in the other without sensibly hurting the regularity of the taper form.

The glasses being chosen and every one marked with a diamond the note you intend it for, they are to be tuned by diminishing the thickness of those that are too sharp. This is done by grinding them round from the neck towards the brim, the breadth of one or two inches, as may be required; often trying the glass by a well-tuned harpsichord, comparing the tone drawn from the glass by your finger, with the note you want, as sounded by that string of the harpsichord. When you come near the matter, be careful to wipe the glass clean and dry before each trial, because the tone is something flatter when the glass is wet, than it will be when dry; and grinding a very little between each trial, you will thereby tune to great exactness. The more care is necessary in this, because if you go below your required tone, there is no sharpening it again but by grinding somewhat off the brim, which will afterwards require polishing, and thus encrease the trouble.

The glasses being thus tuned, you are to be provided with a case for them, and a spindle on which they are to be fixed. (See Plate, Figure 2.) My case is about three feet long, eleven inches every way wide within at the biggest end, and five inches at the smallest end; for it tapers all the way, to adapt it better to the conical figure of the set of glasses. This case opens in the middle of its height, and the upper part turns up by hinges fixed behind. The spindle which is of hard iron, lies horizontally from end to end of the box within, exactly in the middle, and is made to turn on brass gudgeons at each end. It is round, an inch diameter at the thickest end, and tapering to a quarter of an inch at the smallest. A square shank comes from its thickest end through the box, on which shank a wheel is fixed by a screw. This wheel serves as a fly to make the motion equable, when the spindle with the glasses, is turned by the foot like a spinning-wheel. My wheel is of mahogany, 18 inches diameter, and pretty thick, so as to conceal near its circumference about 25 lb of lead. An ivory pin is fixed in the face of this wheel, and about 4 inches from the axis. Over the neck of this pin is put the loop of the string that comes up from the moveable step to give it motion. The case stands on a neat frame with four legs.

To fix the glasses on the spindle, a cork is first to be fitted in each neck pretty tight, and projecting a little without the neck, that the neck of one may not touch the inside of another when put together, for that would make a jarring. These corks are to be perforated with holes of different diameters, so as to suit that part of the spindle on which they are to be fixed. When a glass is put on, by holding it stiffly between both hands, while another turns the spindle, it may be gradually brought to its place. But care must be taken that the hole be not too small, lest, in forcing it up the neck should split; nor too large, lest the glass, not being firmly fixed, should turn or move on the spindle, so as to touch and jar against its neighbouring glass. The glasses thus are placed one in another, the largest on the biggest end of the spindle which is to the left hand; the neck of this glass is towards the wheel, and the next goes into it in the same position, only about an inch of its brim appearing beyond the brim of the first; thus proceeding, every glass when fixed shows about an inch of its brim (or three quarters of an inch, or half an inch, as they grow smaller) beyond the brim of the glass that contains it; and it is from these exposed parts of each glass that the tone is drawn, by laying a finger upon one of them as the spindle and glasses turn round.

My largest glass is G, a little below the reach of a common voice, and my highest G, including three compleat octaves. To distinguish the glasses the more readily to the eye, I have painted the apparent parts of the glasses within side, every semitone white, and the other notes of the octave with the seven prismatic colours, *viz.* C, red; D, orange; E, yellow; F, green; G, blue; A, indigo; B, purple; and C, red again; so that glasses of the same colour (the white excepted) are always octaves to each other.

This instrument is played upon, by sitting before the middle of the set of glasses as before the keys of a harpsichord, turning them with the foot, and wetting them now and then with a spunge and clean water. The fingers should be first a little soaked in water, and quite free from all greasiness; a little fine chalk upon them is sometimes useful, to make them catch the glass and bring out the tone more readily. Both hands are used, by which means different parts are played together. Observe, that the tones are best drawn out when the glasses turn *from* the ends of the fingers, not when they turn *to* them.

The advantages of this instrument are, that its tones are incomparably sweet beyond those of any other; that they may be swelled and softened at pleasure by stronger or weaker pressures of the finger, and continued to any length; and that the instrument, being once well tuned, never again wants tuning.

In honour of your musical language, I have borrowed from it the name of this instrument, calling it the Armonica.

CHAPTER 10

Creator of the Universe

(a) I Believe

Man and his environment always present a critically significant human problem; the most important word is "and", which concerns the relations between man and his environment. Neither can be properly considered isolated from the other. Many people, however, have experienced also the presence of an unseen spirit, God, so that His relations to man and to his environment become even more important.

Franklin's beliefs changed little from his private *Articles of Belief and Acts of Religion*, composed at the age of 22, to the personal letter to Ezra Stiles, written at the age of 84 (6 weeks prior to his death). His creed was based upon belief in "one God, Creator of the Universe." He was evidently an eighteenth-century deist, not strictly a Christian. Deism, however, took various forms: a disinterested God, or a materialistically interested God, or a God morally concerned about the present, or an eternal God of reason—but not of revelation. Franklin believed in the last. One of the most important problems of natural theology, then and now, is the relation of the Creator to His universe. Unfortunately, the pragmatic Franklin was not interested in speculative philosophy, including theology.

To EZRA STILES. *March 9, 1790*

You desire to know something of my Religion. It is the first time I have been questioned upon it. But I cannot take your Curiosity amiss, and shall endeavour in a few Words to gratify it. Here is my

Creed. I believe in one God, Creator of the Universe. That he governs it by his Providence. That he ought to be worshipped. That the most acceptable Service we render to him is doing good to his other Children. That the soul of Man is immortal, and will be treated with Justice in another Life respecting its Conduct in this. These I take to be the fundamental Principles of all sound Religion, and I regard them as you do in whatever Sect I meet with them.

As to Jesus of Nazareth, my Opinion of whom you particularly desire, I think the System of Morals and his Religion, as he left them to us, the best the World ever saw or is likely to see; but I apprehend it has received various corrupting Changes, and I have, with most of the present Dissenters in England, some Doubts as to his Divinity; tho' it is a question I do not dogmatize upon, having never studied it, and think it needless to busy myself with it now, when I expect soon an Opportunity of knowing the Truth with less Trouble. I see no harm, however, in its being believed, if that Belief has the good Consequence, as probably it has, of making his Doctrines more respected and better observed; especially as I do not perceive, that the Supreme takes it amiss, by distinguishing the Unbelievers in his Government of the World with any peculiar Marks of his Displeasure.

I shall only add, respecting myself, that, having experienced the Goodness of that Being in conducting me prosperously thro' a long life, I have no doubt of its Continuance in the next, though without the smallest Conceit of meriting such Goodness. My Sentiments on this Head you will see in the Copy of an old Letter enclosed, which I wrote in answer to one from a zealous Religionist, whom I had relieved in a paralytic case by electricity, and who, being afraid I should grow proud upon it, sent me his serious though rather impertinent Caution. I send you also the Copy of another Letter, which will shew something of my Disposition relation to Religion.

(b) Henceforth Prayers

Franklin did not believe God had created the universe, only to abandon it to its own mechanism. He conceived of God as He Who "governs in the affairs of men." Note that the old word "govern" comes from the same Greek root as our modern cybernetics, i.e. to steer or guide. As we know' in the case of the latter, communication is essential. Needs must be rapidly transmitted in order that the necessary corrections can be made. Such is presumably a function of prayer.

Franklin, the wise old man of the Convention, likened the building of the republic to that of the Tower of Babel, where men strove to reach heaven by their efforts along—without God's help. The builders were unable to work together; the public works project had to be abandoned. He urged Congress to seek "henceforth prayers" before beginning business each morning. Unfortunately prayers require pray-ers.

Franklin wrote on his manuscript: "The Convention, except three or four persons, thought prayers unnecessary."

MOTION FOR PRAYERS IN THE CONVENTION. *June 28, 1787*

MR. PRESIDENT,

The small Progress we have made, after 4 or 5 Weeks' close Attendance and continual Reasonings with each other, our different Sentiments on almost every Question, several of the last producing as many *Noes* as *Ayes*, is, methinks, a melancholy Proof of the Imperfection of the Human Understanding. We indeed seem to *feel* our own want of political Wisdom, since we have been running all about in Search of it. We have gone back to ancient History for Models of Government, and examin'd the different Forms of those Republics, which, having been originally form'd with the Seeds of their own Dissolution, now no longer exist; and we have view'd modern States all round Europe, but find none of their Constitutions suitable to our Circumstances.

In this Situation of this Assembly, groping, as it were, in the dark to find Political Truth, and scarce able to distinguish it when presented to us, how has it happened, Sir, that we have not hitherto once thought of humbly applying to the Father of Lights to illuminate our Understandings? In the Beginning of the Contest with Britain, when we were sensible of Danger, we had daily Prayers in this Room for the Divine Protection. Our Prayers, Sir, were heard; — and they were graciously answered. All of us, who were engag'd in the Struggle, must have observed frequent Instances of a superintending Providence in our Favour. To that kind Providence we owe this happy Opportunity of Consulting in Peace on the Means of establishing our future national Felicity. And have we now forgotten that powerful Friend? or do we imagine we no longer need its assistance? I have lived, Sir, a long time; and the longer I live, the more convincing proofs I see of this Truth, *that* God *governs in the Affairs of Men.* And if a Sparrow cannot fall to the Ground without his Notice, is it probable that an Empire can rise without his Aid? We have been assured, Sir, in the Sacred Writings, that "except the Lord build the House, they labour in vain that build it" I firmly believe this; and I also believe, that, without his concurring Aid, we shall succeed in this political Building no better than the Builders of Babel; we shall be divided by our little, partial, local Interests, our Projects will be confounded, and we ourselves shall become a Reproach and a Bye-word down to future Ages. And, what is worse, Mankind may hereafter, from this unfortunate Instance, despair of establishing Government by human Wisdom, and leave it to Chance, War, and Conquest.

I therefore beg leave to move,

That henceforth Prayers, imploring the Assistance of Heaven and its Blessing on our Deliberations, be held in this Assembly every morning before we proceed to Business; and that one or more of the Clergy of this city be requested to officiate in that Service.

Bibliography

1. ALDRIDGE, ALFRED OWEN, *Benjamin Franklin*, J. B. Lippincott, Philadelphia and New York, 1965.
2. BECKER, CARL LOTUS, *Benjamin Franklin*, Cornell University, Ithaca, 1946.
3. COHEN, I. BERNARD: (a) *Benjamin Franklin's Experiments*, Harvard University, Cambridge, 1941; (b) *Franklin and Newton*, American Philosophical Society, Philadelphia, 1956.
4. CRANE, VERNER W., *Benjamin Franklin and a Rising People* (ed. O. Handlin), Little, Brown, Boston; 1954.
5. (a) *The Autobiography of Benjamin Franklin* (ed. L. W. Labaree *et al.*), Yale University, New Haven and London, 1964.
   (b) *The Papers of Benjamin Franklin* (ed. L. W. Labaree *et al.*), Yale University, New Haven and London, (1960–).
   (c) *The Writings of Benjamin Franklin* (ed. A. H. Smyth), Macmillan, New York, 1906.
   (d) *The Complete Poor Richard Almanacks*, I, II, Imprint Society, Barre, Mass., 1970.
6. PRIESTLEY, JOSEPH, *The History and Present State of Electricity, with Original Experiments* Dudley, Johnson, Payne, Codell, London, 1769.
7. SELLERS, CHARLES COLEMAN, *Benjamin Franklin in Portraiture.* Yale University, New Haven and London, 1962.
8. VAN DOREN, CARL, *Benjamin Franklin*, Viking, New York, 1938.

Name Index

Subject Index